MISHA

MISHA

The Mikhail Baryshnikov Story

Barbara Aria

A 2M Communications Ltd. Production

ST. MARTIN'S PRESS, NEW YORK

MISHA: THE MIKHAIL BARYSHNIKOV STORY. Copyright © 1989 by Barbara
Aria. All rights reserved. Printed in the United States of America. No
part of this book may be used or reproduced in any manner whatsoever
without written permission except in the case of brief quotations embod-
ied in critical articles or reviews. For information, address St. Martin's
Press, 175 Fifth Avenue, New York, N.Y. 10010.

Book design by Judith Stagnitto

Library of Congress Cataloging-in-Publication Data

Aria, Barbara.
    Misha: the Mikhail Baryshnikov story.

    1. Baryshnikov, Mikhail, 1948—   2. Ballet
dancers—Russian S.F.S.R.—Biography.   3. American
Ballet Theatre.   I. Title.
GV1785.B348A77   1989   792.8'2'0924   [B]   88–29845
ISBN 0-312-02610-2

First Edition

10 9 8 7 6 5 4 3 2 1

Contents

Hamlet: Denmark's a prison.

. . . .

Rosencrantz: Why then, your ambition makes it one. 'Tis too
    narrow for your mind.

Hamlet: O God, I could be bounded in a nutshell and count
    myself a king of infinite space, were it not that I have bad
    dreams.

Guildenstern: Which dreams indeed are ambition, for the very
    substance of the ambitious is merely the shadow of a dream.

—Shakespeare, *Hamlet*

MISHA

Flight

 HE HAD DECIDED.

He had been pacing the floor all afternoon, wavering silently, and finally he had decided. He would do it tonight; this was his last chance. It was June 29, 1974, and tonight in Toronto he would lose his past and gain his future. He could scarcely fathom what that really meant.

Tonight twenty-six-year-old Mikhail Baryshnikov, Russia's leading male dancer, cherished son of Leningrad's Kirov Ballet, and inheritor of the world's greatest ballet tradition, would dance his last dance as a Soviet star, slip away from the Bolshoi troupe with which he was touring in Canada, and then defect. He didn't call it defecting, though, he called it selecting, because he had *chosen* it. Choosing was the most painful part.

From there it was all fear and excitement.

Mikhail Baryshnikov was trembling. He was in a strange apartment on the outskirts of Toronto, thousands of miles away from his home in Leningrad. This was a different world: the language was different, the faces were different, life was dif-

1

ferent. And beyond Canada was a whole other world—New York, London, Paris. . . . Where would he go? Would he be a success, so far from home? Tonight he would defect. After that, life would be glaringly unsure.

It was Saturday, and the defection plans had been in place since Thursday. For two days Misha had struggled with the choice, while his friends waited patiently for his final decision. They had watched him pace, knowing the dilemma, knowing that it wasn't the terrible risk of being caught and dragged back to certain imprisonment in Russia that kept him pacing but the fear of losing everything he had and everything he was. Misha was a kid running away from home.

At home Misha was a star. He was loved, he was cared for, he was sheltered. He was given everything he needed—except choices. Until now, at age twenty-six, he had never been faced with the responsibility of choice. He loved his home. Everything about it he would miss terribly. The delicate pastels and frozen skies of his city, the stillness of it, the friends, the fans, the poetry, his dog Foma, the exquisite Kirov stage—each was a part of him. But he was only being chosen for three or four performances a month at the Kirov; he couldn't choose his own roles or partners; he couldn't choose choreographers; he had no choice in where, or when, or what he danced.

Ambition had made the Kirov stage his prison. It was too narrow for his mind; it was suffocating him.

And so he had chosen.

All he had to do now was follow the plan. His *Don Quixote* pas de deux with Irina Kolpakova would be the last dance. When the curtain went down at 10:30 P.M., he would quickly remove his costume and makeup in his dressing room, then leave by the stage door and walk two blocks to a restaurant where Jim Peterson, the Canadian lawyer, would be waiting with a car to drive him back to the apartment. There they would change cars and drive to a safe farmhouse in the country where Misha could hide, prepare a statement, go through the formalities of defec-

tion, and rest. It was so simple, yet when the time came to
return to the theater for his final performance, Misha was trembling like a leaf.

Waiting for curtain call was unbearable. It was almost
time. When it was announced that the performance would be
delayed due to a technical problem, Misha's heart sank. Something was wrong with the curtain mechanism. Just a short delay.
Tonight, of all nights. Five, ten, fifteen minutes. Tonight fifteen
minutes was an unbearable eternity, but finally the curtain
opened, and the lights at the O'Keefe Center dimmed. The
audience was restless. They had been waiting, too, not for
the dancers of the second string Bolshoi troupe but for its guest
star, Mikhail Baryshnikov. There were rumors that he was a
genius.

And genius he was. When Baryshnikov first stepped onto the
stage, the audience saw only the boyish face, more cute than
handsome, and the small, stocky body—nothing exceptional.
But the moment he moved to dance, his whole image was transformed. Behind the radiant energy of the dancing Baryshnikov,
no sign of the trembling Misha remained. His two *Nutcracker* pas
de deux with the brilliant Kolpakova were of unparalleled grace,
and his pas de deux from *Don Quixote*—wild, devilish, forceful—
was inspired bravura.

It was already 10:30 when Misha stepped onto the stage for
that last pas de deux, and he danced as if there was no tomorrow.

The audience went wild. Ovations kept coming, Misha
bowed, the stage filled with flowers, Misha bowed again, the
ballerinas curtsied, the company bowed, Misha bowed, and still
the audience wanted more. Misha was desperate. He felt the
minutes slipping by. After fifteen minutes for the opening curtain and another fifteen trapped on stage by ecstatic fans, he was
afraid the car might have already left.

As the applause faded, Misha dashed backstage toward his
dressing room. Halfway there he was stopped. He was told that

there was to be a reception right after the show and that the whole troupe must attend. He was being told to change quickly and meet the others outside the stage door, where a bus would be waiting to take the dancers to the reception.

Misha saw the bus as he left the theater through the stage door in his street clothes. He also saw the crowd of fans beginning to surround him. Some of his colleagues were already on the bus, waiting. They saw him. Fans were closing in on him, holding out autograph books. He could sign a couple, board the bus, and forget the whole thing. He could go home, safe and sound. Impulsively, he broke into a run. The crowd of fans provided a few moments of cover.

"When I started to run, I didn't feel my legs under me, I just felt fear and empty stomach." He could hear the dancers shouting from the bus, "Misha, where are you going!" And he realized that some fans were following him, running after him with their autograph books. Pure adrenaline moved him—he was outrunning his fans, but he didn't know where he was going. Without stopping, he ran into the street, heard a car screech, and realized he had almost been hit. Still running, he crossed a dark lot. Nothing looked familiar. He was lost, but his legs kept pumping.

Parked outside the restaurant, Peterson figured he had waited long enough. Maybe Misha had changed his mind, or perhaps he'd been stopped. He got out of the car and started toward the theater to see what he could find out. But then through the darkness he saw someone racing toward him. It was Misha; he was running like prey, helpless and unseeing. Peterson hailed a passing cab. "I almost threw up when I jumped into that car," Misha remembers. He was shaking, white with fear and exhaustion.

That night they drank vodka and laughed. They felt exhilarated. They had done it—*he* had done it. Baryshnikov was free.

It was a strange sensation, freedom. It was exciting, and it was scary. All over Europe, in every major ballet company, doors were open for him. He could go anywhere, do anything. He could choose. He could make mistakes. He might lose himself.

Misha drank and laughed, and drank and cried. He was very excited and very scared. This was altogether a new experience.

TWO

Boy
Baryshnikov

WHEN MIKHAIL BARYSHNIKOV, at the age of twenty-six, chose to make his new home in the West, he came not as an immigrant with bags full of favorite trinkets and best suits, but as a defector with nothing but the clothes on his back and memories of a Soviet boyhood. In the months ahead, the bones of these memories would be unburied again and again by reporters, admirers, and would-be friends seeking the person behind the persona—the "Russian soul" of Baryshnikov. It was not an easy search. Misha's past was submerged in a part of himself he considered private; after all, what did his boyhood have to do with his dancing?

The Baryshnikov family had no former connection with the world of dance. Mikhail's father, Nikolai Baryshnikov, was a military topographer; his mother, Alexandra Kiseleva, was a seamstress in a fashion house. Theirs was a fairly ordinary, middle-class Russian family enjoying the relative comforts of life in the new Soviet republic of Latvia. Like their neighbors, they worked hard, were secure in their jobs, and earned an average wage that provided them with all of the necessities in life plus an occasional frivolity. There wasn't much excitement, but they didn't have to worry about their next meal.

Nikolai and Alexandra had met soon after World War II, in the great Volga River region where Alexandra had grown up. Both had been married before. Alexandra's husband had been killed at the front, leaving her with a young son to care for; Nikolai had a daughter from a previous marriage. Misha doubts that there was ever any great romance in his parents' relationship—their courtship was "rather quick, I think." Marriage must have been a convenient solution for them both. For the young Alexandra, a widowed, penniless young woman with a dependent son and mother and no job, it was a question of surviving through the grim days of postwar Russia. For Nikolai, marriage meant not having to live alone. "My father couldn't live alone," says Misha.

On January 27, 1948—Mozart's birthday—Mikhail Nikolaivich was born into a family at odds with itself. Nikolai had effectively shut himself off from Alexandra and her son, Mikhail's eight-year-old half brother. His half sister lived in Leningrad.

"I felt the tension from very early on," Misha remembers. Unable to bridge the gap that divided them, his parents fought. They came from different worlds. His father was an intensely serious, well-educated man from a family that had owned a factory. He had become a devout Stalinist, and by the time Misha was born he was a high-ranking military commander teaching topography in the air force academy. He was a man of steel— hard, taut, liable to snap. Mikhail's mother, on the other hand, was a bright and intuitive but uneducated country girl from a peasant family.

While young Mikhail grew up, his father worked and read. He would come home from the academy and withdraw behind the pages of one of the books from his vast library of classics. And there he would sit, inaccessibly, into the night, falling asleep in his chair, until he woke for work in the morning. Whether his father absorbed any of the poetry or passion in the literature he read, Mikhail does not know. He never showed any tenderness. Misha couldn't get close to him. They saw each other at breakfast and before Misha went to bed. Nikolai always wore his military uniform, even on family outings.

Misha was very much his mother's son. He had her full, open face, her ash blond hair, her large, clear blue eyes and heavy lids. She was beautiful, and she always took care to make herself look nice. Misha loved her. He loved her quickness and her sense of fantasy. She was very physical, and so was he. He was a small, serious boy surrounded by unhappiness.

Misha's relationship with the world beyond his family was no easier. Riga, where he was born and grew up, was the capital city of Latvia, a tiny, proud country just across the Baltic Sea from Sweden, that had been struggling for independence from one or another invading force since the twelfth century. After having been ruled by Germany, Poland, Sweden, and Russia, Latvia saw a few years of independence between the world wars, only to be occupied by Germany, handed over to Stalin as part of the Russo-German nonaggression pact of 1939, retaken by Hitler's forces in 1941, and finally, in 1945, only three years before Misha's birth, reclaimed by Stalin. After the war Latvia reluctantly became a republic of the Soviet Union.

As the son of a Russian military officer, Misha had a hard time making friends in Riga; "My parents were considered aggressors." Although Misha spoke fluent Latvian, he and his family were visibly different. The Latvians were closer in physique and temperament to their Scandinavian neighbors than to their Russian invaders. The Latvians were cosmopolitan; they wore tailored European clothes. The Russians looked drab and provincial by comparison. So Misha made friends with other kids who were set apart in one way or another—some were Jews, some were the children of Latvian artists or musicians. But Misha didn't feel comfortable inviting his friends home because his father, who hated both Latvians and Jews, might insult them and embarrass Misha. "Somehow it forced me to . . . masquerade." Among his friends, a playful, witty Misha began to emerge.

For the child whose family life is tense or unhappy, home is not a haven. When the atmosphere begins to thicken, he will escape to the outdoors, where the air is clear and he can run and kick and jump away the weight he felt at home. Every gang, every club, every sport and after-school activity becomes an excuse to stay away. So it was with Misha. He enjoyed being active, using his body, using physical space. He hated to sit still.

The Soviet state provides a huge range of opportunities for children eager to learn something new or develop their talents— "If you're good in school, do your homework, have decent marks, you could be busy twenty-four hours a day," remembers Misha—and Misha was eager. These were nonacademic, optional activities provided for free, yet they were intended as serious pursuits. The state sought excellence, and the children knew that it was ready to nurture its best talents regardless of a family's encouragement, income, or position.

From the age of six or seven Misha learned to channel his youthful, nervous energy into physical disciplines. He took gymnastics and soccer. He excelled in fencing, and he ran. What he lacked in ability to concentrate, Misha made up for in sheer mental and physical agility and enthusiasm. During the summer months he swam determinedly in the cold Baltic Sea. In lonelier moments, Misha fished.

Even family life was more comfortable when it was conducted out of doors. Misha's best boyhood memories are of family outings and vacations. There were pleasant Sundays, when the Baryshnikovs would become a typical Russian family on a woodland excursion. Bundled up in winter scarves and suits, stopping for a balmy spring picnic, or sifting with sticks through the blazing leaves of fall, the family would forage for wild mushrooms in the nearby woods along with other parents and children and the old *babushkas*. By the end of the weekend the woods would be picked clean. A family snapshot shows the young Baryshnikov, in baggy pants and sweater, grinning face topped with a mop of blond hair, proudly holding out a mushroom while his other hand carries a brimming basketful.

For a week or two during the summer the family would rent a beach house. Misha would swim, and his father would put aside his uniform. "He was a different man. But still, he walked like he was in uniform."

Mikhail's fervent athleticism was almost matched by his love for music. He loved to listen to it, and he wanted to make it. He joined the children's choir and delighted in the glorious concert of voices he helped to make. He wanted to learn to play the piano. He had it in his mind that he wanted to become a great concert pianist. He could see himself, up there on the stage, the beautiful wood and ivory of the grand piano glowing in a pool of light, his fingers dancing lightly over the keys while the orchestra soared, producing its magic.

But Misha wasn't a brilliant pianist. He was good—good enough to enjoy playing around on the keyboard. Yet, whether it was because he didn't have the patience to sit and master scales and arpeggios or because he expected too much too soon, somehow Misha knew that the piano was not to be his destiny.

Alexandra, too, loved music; her voice itself was "like melody." She was instinctively drawn to beauty. She needed some form of escape from a suffocating marriage and what she felt to be the endless drabness of her life. Her refuge lay in the splendors of the theater, opera, and ballet. She couldn't understand the words of the operas she heard, as she'd had no cultural education. She was simply thrilled by the sound and the spectacle. Usually Alexandra would attend these performances alone, but occasionally she took Misha. He was her boy; he liked music.

Of course, it was wonderful for Misha to accompany his mother on such outings. She would be looking beautiful in one of her nicest dresses, her eyes shining with enjoyment; the elegant theater on Padomiju Boulevard would be glittering with lights. It was a world of fantasy. Misha found it hard to sit still through a whole opera. Not so with the ballet, however, because there are "more colors there, and people moving." He saw *Don Quixote*, whose pas de deux he was to dance on the night of his defection, and he saw *Giselle*, that great romance of love and betrayal with which the name Baryshnikov would come to be identified.

Misha could hardly compare what he saw at the ballet with the kind of dance he did after school, when a group of children would meet for an hour of folk dancing. This was just another extracurricular activity, and its attraction lay mainly in music and in girls. "You go, and it's music playing, and everybody's learning to dance, and you have to hold her in your arms. . . ." Most of the time, girls his age giggled in groups or pretended to be engaged in serious study. Here was an opportunity to get close to a girl and, while close, charm her with talk. And Misha was good at this.

The ballet was different. It involved music, of course—huge, magnificent music—and it involved romance. It was also clear to Misha that there were stories being told, stories of princes and peasants and grand passions. In the classical ballets that he saw, Misha was introduced to a cultural relic—a relic of the days before the vast social revolution that had built schools and factories and railroad trestles, that had raised everyday work to heroic levels.

Classical ballet was pure frivolity. However much the social messages of aristocratic degeneracy were emphasized in works like *Giselle*, ballet had nothing to do with the kind of patriotism represented by Nikolai Baryshnikov. Everyone knew that the czars had promoted the development of ballet for their own entertainment and that for years the czars' dancers had been their privileged serfs, transported to the theater nightly in golden carriages with locked doors. The Revolution had opened the theaters to the people, and in the name of the people the tradition of classical ballet—the rightful heritage of the proletariat—was preserved.

But to preserve meant to protect from change, and so while bridges and factories and schools were built, the classical ballets created for an aristocracy were faithfully, changelessly performed. Now, in the sprawling Soviet city of Riga, the world of ballet remained a world by itself, a world seemingly untouched by party or politics, a piece of fantasy. For many like Alexandra Kiseleva, ballet at the old theater on Padomiju Boulevard seemed to represent, as Joseph Brodsky called it, "the art of better days."

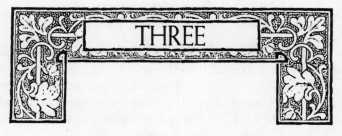

THREE

First
Pirouettes
and Sorrow

 HAD MIKHAIL BARYSHNIKOV been born and raised in one of the many remote, shapeless provinces of the vast Soviet state, he might never have been introduced to his first pirouette. For while Riga is a provincial city, it is by no means a cultural backwater.

In the sixteenth century, Peter the Great made his home in Riga, and with him came the aristocracy. Over time, a long history of invasions from Europe made Riga seem more like a Western European city than the historically isolated cities of the Soviet Union. Its fine port and waterways attracted trade, and with trade came a broad sphere of influence. By the middle of the nineteenth century Riga was already developing into the large, industrial city that Misha inhabited as a boy. Misha's Riga was a thriving, cosmopolitan metropolis with a rich cultural legacy.

Riga possessed all the marks of man's strivings to create phys-

13

ical beauty by taming and shaping the raw materials of nature. There was the once-walled medieval old town, with its gothic spires rising high into the sky and its streets so narrow that, standing with arms outstretched, Misha could almost touch the houses on either side; the intricate, baroque mansions of the merchants; the romance of seventy nineteenth-century palaces that lined the canals; the swirling decoration of art nouveau facades; the symmetry of the stately parks, with their rose gardens and waterfalls; the broad, leafy boulevards; the pure lines of classical columns; the massive, ancient trees. In this environment of rich forms, the young Baryshnikov began to develop a sure sense of beauty and style that might otherwise have lain dormant.

When Misha was twelve he decided take the exam for admission to the School of Opera and Ballet Theater in Riga. It was a sudden impulse. He'd watched the ballet, he liked folk dancing, he was as athletic as the male dancers he'd seen on stage, and he wasn't going to make it as a concert pianist. In Russia, ballet for boys didn't hold the kind of connotations that it held in the West at that time. Russian men danced, by tradition; even the Red Army has its permanent unit of dancers. Music and dance are as Russian as frescos are Italian. The Revolution didn't destroy the ballet, despite its aristocratic heritage. Instead, the Soviet program of social realism made ballet dancing more athletic. The Russian male dancer triumphed and so did Russian ballet.

Whether the idea of a ballet career was initially Misha's or his mother's is unclear. It certainly was not his father's idea. Nikolai had assumed that his son would study hard and take up some steady, useful profession—becoming a pilot or an engineer, perhaps. The boy was strong and bright, and he had every opportunity to make something of himself by participating in the building and rebuilding of the nation which was still so crucial in the postwar years.

Despite his father's misgivings, Mikhail went ahead with his plan. He wasn't attracted to science or technology as were so many optimistic young Russians of the previous generation. Nor was he interested in politics, good citizenry, or the "heroism of everyday work" that his father had espoused. After all, Misha was of a very different generation, a postwar generation formed in the years of political thaw heralded by Nikita Khrushchev. It was 1960. In the West, "generation gap" had just been defined and there existed a new youth culture. The war and its austere aftermath were over. In Russia, bridges and schools and factories had been built, man had orbited in space, and Stalin had been temporarily divested of glory. Yet essentially, nothing seemed to have changed. The old order prevailed. Young people of Misha's generation were tending to sidestep the system rather than to serve it. Ballet, and the arts in general, had become one kind of sidestep.

At the age of twelve Misha wasn't seriously questioning the system, but he did feel the prevailing atmosphere. Ballet had become popular among independent-minded young Russians, such as the rebellious young Rudolf Nureyev, who was now dancing on the Kirov stage. Ballet was an attractive alternative with colorful traditions that crossed historical and political boundaries. And Riga had an excellent ballet institute.

Besides, Mikhail wasn't doing well in school. Although he was conscientious in his studies, he'd always had trouble concentrating. It was a struggle for him to sit still at his desk in class. And while he could deal with the dramas of history and literature, the cool abstractions of math had become torturous. He'd begun to cheat and lie about his homework because he couldn't, or wouldn't, do it, and he was embarrassing his father. Nikolai Baryshnikov was very keen on hard work and self-discipline.

Nevertheless, Mikhail's announcement at age twelve that "next Tuesday" he was going to take an exam for professional ballet

school came out of the blue. He hadn't been yearning for classical dance, as Nureyev had yearned in faraway Ufa. In addition,
many would have already considered him too old to begin serious training—most boys start at age eight or nine, when both
muscles and wills are still soft and pliable. In an October 8, 1987
Rolling Stone interview with Nancy Collins, Baryshnikov claims
that his was more of a "career choice" than a passion. "If you
were dancing professionally, it was good money, security,
twenty years of guaranteed work, trips abroad, privileges and a
pension."

This is a surprisingly dispassionate way for a twelve year old,
on the brink of one of the most emotional ages in a boy's life, to
look at his future. But if Misha really did have a steady career in
mind, the Riga dance school, with its historic ties to the Kirov,
was just the place to start. The Riga Choreographic Institute was
attached to the reputable Latvian State Opera and Ballet Theater, the same company whose productions Misha had watched
on Padomiju Boulevard. The theater was opened in 1919, two
days after the Red Army took Latvia from the Germans; its
school was founded in the late twenties by the Kirov ballerina
Alexandra Fedorova, sister-in-law of the legendary Michel
Fokine. She brought the best of the classics from Leningrad and
trained a generation of young Latvians. Some of Misha's teachers
had been students of Fedorova. Like all Soviet ballet schools,
the Riga curriculum was based on the teachings of Agrippina
Vaganova, the legendary Kirov teacher after whom the Kirov's
ballet school is named and whose system has produced some of
the world's greatest ballet dancers. Vaganova's book *Fundamentals
of the Classic Dance* (1934) has become the bible of twentieth-
century Russian ballet education.

In his first year at the Riga dance school Baryshnikov was
introduced to the severe discipline of ballet. He started in the
beginners' class. Since the Riga course was designed to be completed over a nine-year period, Misha could expect to become a

professional dancer at the age of twenty-one—assuming, as was usually the case for dancers, that he was exempted from the normal period of military service. That was a long stretch of time ahead, and Misha must have quickly realized what hard work those years would be.

School days were split between academic classes and classes in the basic grammar of classical ballet—one and a half hours a day of pure, disciplined exercise which involved endless memorizing of French names for steps and positions. Later, classes in character dance were added. Students were kept busy practicing pliés or leaps in one of the two huge rooms of the old dance school, then running across the square for a math or art history class at the academic school they shared with children from the nearby music conservatory, back across the square for more ballet method, back again for literature or French, and so on, all day long, until their young minds and bodies were exhausted. Misha also took lessons in piano, music, and fencing. There was hardly any time to play, and after a while Misha began to wish that he could run around the streets of Riga with the other boys. He was envious of their gangs, their tough-guy stance. He wanted to be Riff, his young hero from *West Side Story*. But Misha knew that in order to succeed, he had to give all of that up.

In the beginning young Baryshnikov wasn't sure if he would make it as a dancer. His first teacher, Natalia Leontyeva, had her doubts, too. His physique didn't fit the profile of a male dancer. He was stocky, his head and hands were too large for his body, and he didn't have that spring in his feet that comes naturally to some boys. Worst of all, he was short. "How are you going to lift a partner?" Misha's teachers would ask. Alexander Godunov, Misha's Riga classmate who became a Bolshoi star and later joined him in exile, had the same problem. Misha and Alexander were always competing, always driving each other to do better. Even growing became a competition. Together they tried every remedy their school friends recommended, from drinking large amounts of tomato juice to sleeping on hard boards. For a while Misha was winning, but then Alexander grew again.

Misha was as fanatical about his slightly inturned pelvis as he was about his height. To correct it, he subjected himself to the agonizing process of stretching his pelvic ligaments. "I would sit in a yogalike position and ask people to sit on my knees," he remembers. For weeks the pain was almost unbearable. It hurt even when he lay down to sleep. But Misha knew that as a ballet dancer he would have to learn to tolerate pain, just as he had to accept the rigid discipline of class and the endless hours of work. Ballet is an unnatural discipline; the body must adjust to movements and positions that are not normal for human beings. For the ballet dancer, pain is a constant reality.

Baryshnikov's zeal won out over appearances. He may have looked odd, but he had immense energy, even for his age, and his young muscles were already powerful. Misha's dance teachers were impressed. He had a natural feeling for music. He was quick and responsive, too, a smart kid who learned with ease. He absorbed information quickly, always eager to move on to the next challenge. It was a joy for Misha to be dancing. His teacher in character dance, Bella Kovarskaya, remembers the way he radiated: "You were so excited about teaching when you saw his face. He was bright." Misha was also ambitious; he wanted to be the best.

When Baryshnikov speaks of his years at the Riga dance school it is almost as if home didn't exist. What was happening in that tense house while Misha learned to pirouette? About that Baryshnikov is evasive, preferring instead to talk about dance. However, somewhere around the end of his first year of dance school his mother disappears from his story. What was happening in Baryshnikov's life as he learned to be a dancer? His mother left, he said, abandoning him. He has told friends of the enduring pain of abandonment. In another of his accounts his mother fell sick and died. Reluctantly, he reveals the truth: his mother committed suicide. She hanged herself. He didn't know the truth at the time, he knew only that she had died. Misha felt abandoned, wounded. Although he covered up the hurt, it's a wound that friends say has never healed.

Mikhail had been staying with his grandmother, his mother's mother, in her village near the Volga River. He was there for the summer vacation, a long way from Riga and school. When Nikolai's telegram came, Mikhail, his grandmother, and his uncle traveled two days by train to get to Riga for the funeral. It was a typical Russian funeral, with the casket open. Mikhail walked with the procession. The orchestra played a funeral march based on a Chopin sonata. It was "spooky" and sad, but Misha says he accepted his mother's death. Life went on. Already he was beginning to feel that Riga was a small place, that he would have to move on.

After the funeral Alexandra's mother stayed on to take care of Nikolai and Mikhail. Mikhail went back to school. This was his second year at the Riga dance school, and he had committed himself absolutely to becoming a dancer. He immersed himself completely. He had been transferred to the intermediate class of Yuris Kapralis, a young dancer in the Latvian company with a gift for teaching. "He was a great methodist," recalls Baryshnikov. "He introduced me to the idea of how difficult it is to learn something, and how easy it is when you want to do something." Kapralis appreciated Mikhail's zestfulness. The boy was fun and easygoing—his was the smiling face in class—yet he was serious, too. Kapralis was struck by his intellectual approach to dance. And Mikhail liked his teacher. Kapralis was very smart. When you have a special relationship with a teacher, you flourish. Baryshnikov was getting straight fives in class, five being the highest grade.

In his third year Misha was moved to the advanced class. The stage was already in his blood. Children from the school had been dancing with the ballet company, and Misha was being given at least one part a week, the best of the children's parts in ballets like *The Sleeping Beauty* and *The Nutcracker*. The experience corrupted him. As he recalls in an interview with Nancy Collins, "the orchestra, the lights, the smell of makeup and powder," and the feeling of being someone very special had him hooked in no time at all. Now Misha knew for sure that he wanted to be a ballet dancer.

The theater and classes became Mikhail's life. In his mind, he had already left home. Nikolai was adjusting to his son's chosen career, mainly because of the boy's obvious ability. He remarried, and even though Misha got along with his stepmother, home didn't feel right. It contained a lingering sadness; it was empty for him. The theater felt more like his kind of home. The theater was a family in which he occupied a special place.

Misha's teacher, Bella Kovarskaya, recognized his ambitions and his potential. "The dancing went out of him," she remembers. "He was perfect in everything that he did." Kovarskaya's realm was acting. At fourteen Misha was already technically outstanding, but it wasn't enough just to have "capable legs"; a dancer had to act, to project. To compensate for his build, Misha needed what his teacher called a "noble carriage." Kovarskaya still credits herself with having developed in her student a firm sense of presence to match his leaps.

When Baryshnikov was fifteen Kovarskaya created a solo for him—the male solo in *Tarantella*, to music by Rossini. It is the greatest of honors for a dancer to have a role choreographed on him. Baryshnikov danced with two little girl ballerinas, and his performance was met with roaring applause. As Kovarskaya remembers, "Everyone said, 'what a charming boy! How musical he is!'" This was Baryshnikov's first solo.

Later that year Kovarskaya was sent to Leningrad for a

special program in dance education. She went to the Vaganova school of the Kirov Ballet, where she taught and studied. She made a special effort to observe the classes of Alexander Pushkin, the remarkable teacher who had recently nurtured the talents of Rudolf Nureyev. While she was there Kovarskaya talked to Pushkin about her exceptional young student, Baryshnikov.

FOUR

Leningrad

NEWS SPREADS QUICKLY in ballet circles. From city to city, company to company, and teacher to teacher, the stories travel—stories of budding talents, fading stars, new partnerships. Before Mikhail Baryshnikov even knew about a trip to Leningrad, the ballet circles in Leningrad had heard about Baryshnikov, that "outstanding boy" at the Riga dance school.

It was 1964, three years since Nureyev's defection in Paris, and balletomanes were yearning for a new young star to fill the void. When the editor at Leningrad Television found out that young Mikhail Baryshnikov would be dancing in town with the Latvian company he told the cameraman to be sure and focus on the "future genius."

Mikhail Baryshnikov was almost sixteen. He was a boy with three years of serious dance school experience, a boy still struggling with math lessons, a boy who knew that at some point he would be leaving Latvia for something bigger and better. When he heard that he would be touring with the Latvian Opera and

Ballet Theater in Leningrad, he saw the opportunity for what it was. Misha had already thought about Leningrad, home of the Kirov Ballet and its Vaganova Institute, the best ballet school in the world. Bella Kovarskaya had advised him to pay a visit to the teacher, Alexander Pushkin. Misha's stepsister lived in Leningrad; he had thought about visiting her there, mainly so that he could visit the Vaganova school. But now he actually was going to Leningrad, where he would be dancing the part of the Young Boy with the Bow in the ballet *Shakuntala*. This was not one of the insignificant little children's parts, either, it was a solo in the Latvian Ballet's latest hit production.

Leningrad is a full day's journey east and north from Riga—just a stone's throw in the vast expanses of the Soviet Union, yet it is a world apart, and always has been. Countless visitors to Leningrad have been enraptured by the city's splendor, by its serene beauty and elegance and a kind of magical quality that fills the air. "Another age! Another country! Another world!" wrote choreographer Agnes de Mille when she arrived in Leningrad from Moscow with the touring American Ballet Theatre in 1966. "It is a city transfixed," she said, "opalescent beside its still canals, pearly, pink and touched with gold against the sky." For Misha, too, it was love at first sight. This was the most beautiful place he had ever seen. Riga's palaces and canals and boulevards paled by comparison with those of Leningrad. But it wasn't only the beauty. The city *felt* different. This was the home of art; this was Russia's Paris, its Venice. Everything about it seemed to speak the homage of men and women to beauty. The city was a vision of perfectly contemplated order and harmony.

Leningrad is both the birthplace of ballet in Russia and an image of the ballet itself—like the ballet, its lines are supremely classical and exquisitely restrained. It is a city created by the aristocracy, a fabulous stage set for their courtly lives. Its sumptuous palaces, golden cupolas, marble statues, and painted facades rise out of the snow, glowing in the clear, pale northern light. Leningrad was founded by Peter the Great as a "bridge to the West," an antidote to Russia's stubborn cultural isolation. When the promised "bridge" failed to materialize, Peter's jester wryly renamed it a "window to the West," a name still used today. Leningrad was Peter's dream, but the city's most magnificent buildings and streets were commissioned later, by empresses who were turning green with envy over Louis XIV's palace at Versailles.

For Misha, Leningrad was cultural history come alive. Here was the St. Petersburg Conservatory, where Tchaikovsky studied and played his first concerts; here were the homes of Pushkin, Dostoevsky, Tolstoy, and Chekhov, the houses in which were written the classics of Russian literature. And the whole place was imbued with ballet. Tchaikovsky wrote some of the greatest ballet scores in Leningrad, and Dostoevsky's and Pushkin's stories had become the stories of ballets. Here was the pistachio-green, art nouveau palace built by the Grand Duke Andrei for his new wife and princess, the great Kirov ballerina Mathilda Kschessinska. When the aristocracy fell, Lenin spoke from her balcony and established party headquarters in the ballerina's deserted palace.

But the most magnificent piece of ballet history that Misha saw was the Kirov school building on Rossi Street, once the Imperial Ballet School of St. Petersburg, now the Vaganova Choreographic Institute. Here were contained two-hundred years of tradition—all the ballet history Mikhail had been studying in school. Rossi Street (originally Theatre Street, as immortalized in ballerina Tamara Karsavina's memoirs) is one of the most perfect tributes to classical beauty ever achieved on such a small scale.

Created by the great Florentine architect Carlo Rossi, son of an Italian ballerina and a Russian father, Ulitsa Rossi is a short, spacious street, a peaceful cul-de-sac flanked for its entire length by the Central Theatre Museum on one side and the Vaganova school on the other. The two buildings are identical, each with its long, serene ocher-pink facade punctuated by bold white columns. The height of the buildings is identical to the width of the street, and the street's length is exactly ten times its width. "Dancing and building are the two primary and essential arts," Havelock Ellis once said, "and in the end they unite." Supremely classical, Rossi Street must have been a daily inspiration for the students of the Vaganova Institute.

Alexander Minz was a Kirov dancer when the young Baryshnikov came to Leningrad for the first time. Minz still remembers seeing Misha perform with the Riga Ballet company and being astonished by the boy's superb technical mastery and strong stage presence. But when Baryshnikov thinks back to his first trip to Leningrad, it is his visit to the legendary Vaganova school that stands out in his memories. This was what he'd been waiting for. Every young dancer in the country must have dreamed of trying out for the Vaganova school, and here he was, in the very building that had once been the Imperial Ballet School; here he was, walking through the very door that George Balanchine once walked through, standing in the grand, wood-paneled hallway where Sergei Pavlovich Diaghilev himself had stood, climbing the marble stairs that Vaslav Nijinsky once climbed, and entering the same palatial studio where Rudolf Nureyev had studied not so long ago with the same Alexander Pushkin who he was now to meet.

Pushkin, a classical dancer renowned for his incredible leaps, had been a dancer at the Kirov for almost thirty years. From the age of twenty-five he had also taught, and during that time he had become a legend in the world of ballet training. To Misha, he was a large man of fifty-six with an odd face, a big belly, a gentle manner, and a cultured way of speaking, a man who seemed to have "stepped out of an icon." This was the teacher who had trained some of the best male dancers in the Soviet Union.

Pushkin asked very little of Mikhail Baryshnikov. The boy had already been introduced to him as an exceptional student by his teacher, Bella Kovarskaya. Instead of making him run through endless exercises, Pushkin just felt his leg muscles and asked him to jump. Misha remembers, "I was like a young goat, knocking over tables and chairs." But Pushkin must have been satisfied. He sent him to see the school doctor—standard practice for all potential students—and personally accepted him into his seventh-year class for boys. Misha returned to Riga and spent the summer waiting anxiously for official acceptance to the Vaganova school. He knew the competition was fierce; after all, this was the best and most famous school in the whole world for classical ballet. When the waiting grew to be too much, Misha went fishing.

Word finally came. Mikhail Baryshnikov was privileged to be accepted into Alexander Ivanovich Pushkin's seventh-year class at the Agrippina Vaganova Leningrad Choreographic Institute. Misha's sense of relief was enormous. He had savored Leningrad, he had felt the serenity of Rossi Street and seen all that the Vaganova school offered, and during those long summer hours in Riga he had known that this school was his greatest hope. There could be no second best; everything else was nothing compared to this.

Mikhail returned to Leningrad, to the fine old studios and classrooms of the Vaganova school, to the faint taste of privilege that still clung to the long, peeling corridors. Now it was real—he was a part of it. The hallways were his, as were the courtyards cluttered with bicycles, and the spare, functional dressing rooms that contained his locker and a place for him to change into tights and shoes on one of the hard wooden benches. The beautiful third-floor miniature theater was his, as were the winding stairways and landings, wiped and polished each day by an army of cleaning ladies, and the little fifth-floor museum where he could go to absorb ballet history through the memories of its supervisor, Maria-Marietta Frangopolo, and her collections of photographs showing past students turned great dancers. And the main studio was his, this room of grand proportions with its sharply raked wooden floor corresponding exactly to the slant of the Kirov stage. Here he would take his lessons with Pushkin, before the vast mirrors at either end, with two stories of airy space about him, and with two windows framing views of tranquil greenery. The sculptured busts of the legendary teacher Agrippina Vaganova and the great choreographer Marius Petipa would watch over his progress from either side of the gallery overhanging the studio.

All of this now belonged to Baryshnikov, and it didn't take him long to understand that he would have to work intensely to hold on to it. Vaganova students were privileged, but not by birthright. The school, like all Soviet schools, was entirely state supported; students were there at the expense of a society that treasured its tradition of excellence. Vaganova students could be expelled, thrown back to a life of meager status for any number of reasons. The intense competition that Mikhail had faced when he applied for admission, he realized, would continue throughout his training.

"Leningrad was a shock. I had to work from eight in the morning till eleven at night, and pass all exams: French, geometry, piano lessons." In the beginning, Baryshnikov didn't think he would make it. Life at the Vaganova Institute was like a test of the student's devotion to dance, almost a monastic apprenticeship. Anna Pavlova herself described it as "a convent whence frivolity is banned, and where merciless discipline reigns," and Nijinsky spoke of "the discipline of military drill." Only the true believer would suffer the rigors it demanded.

FIVE

Working Days

 VAGANOVA STUDENTS WERE given nothing but the best. Besides the most complete dance training in the world and all of the necessary clothing and equipment, they were provided with the same academic education given to all students in Soviet schools. The academic classes were known as "sitting subjects," and most of the ballet students resented them, particularly when they were still tired from the extreme physical exertions of dance.

Misha's mornings began with two to three hours of intense training in classical ballet; boys and girls took dance classes separately. Then there was just enough time for him to change out of his tights and shift into academic gear. Since the Vaganova elevator was for staff use only, getting to the next class might mean running from a third-floor studio to a second-floor changing room and then getting back up to the fifth floor for class, all within ten minutes. There was rarely time to peek in on the studios where the Kirov stars came to rehearse, yet the students felt their presence in the school and were awed by them.

The change from the large, open studio to the confines of the classroom was difficult in itself. "The first door off one of the Academy's endless passageways opened to the studio for our daily classes," describes another former Vaganova student, Valery Panov, in his autobiography *To Dance*. "The following ones were to the smaller classrooms with their prisonlike rows of desks." At these desks Mikhail and about forty other dancers sat struggling with their schoolwork. Each time the bell rang it was time to switch again, from geometry, to history, to literature, to Soviet constitution, and so on. Another Vaganova student, Natalia Makarova, remembers feeling like a "wind-up toy." "Hardly any going out with girls," recalls Misha, "there was no time."

These general subjects were not treated lightly by the administration. Academic standards were high—higher than those required for an American high school diploma. Like most of the students, Mikhail tackled his studies diligently, because he was determined to succeed as a dancer. There was no way to avoid it. He couldn't graduate from Vaganova without having first passed exams in the academic curriculum. Dancers, even these chosen few, were expected to be broadly educated.

The classes in humanities—literature, music, and art history—were the least problematic for Misha. He loved to read, and books gave him an important aesthetic education that would allow him to delve fully into the roles of each ballet he would perform—into its history, its music, its poetry. By far the most popular "sitting subject" was ballet history. This class was given in the little fifth-floor museum by its supervisor, Maria-Marietta Frangopolo. An elderly Frenchwoman of great charm, Mme Frangopolo had been a Kirov dancer for thirty years and a colleague of Balanchine in his Leningrad days, and her lessons in ballet history were always enlivened by personal recollections. Surrounded by walls of memorabilia and immersed in the traditions of Russian ballet, she and her students would look through albums of photographs and volumes of ballet magazines—including a few rare prerevolutionary periodicals and some generally unobtainable Western magazines, which Misha remembers as having been something like a dancer's *The Gulag Archipelago.* Frangopolo could answer questions on any number of obscure ballet subjects; she even could offer some sketchy information on ballet trends in the West—trends that were dismissed in the curriculum of this citadel of tradition as "lifeless," "bourgeois," and "corrupt." Mme Frangopolo was also an expert in affairs of the heart and reputedly gave frequent and valuable advice to young, lovesick students.

After "sitting subjects" and a quick, scrappy lunch in the school cafeteria came the bell and time to change back into tights for classes in character dance and mime. These classes were a crucial aspect of Russian ballet training, an aspect that is virtually ignored in the West. Through his teacher, Igor Belsky, the Kirov's leading character dancer, Baryshnikov learned how to make his technically perfect movements speak, how to tell a story without words. A performer first and teacher second, Belsky was a live spark whose untidy but inspired approach to classes caught the imagination of his best students. He taught by example. He would perform pieces from his incredible repertoire of roles, showing how a single movement could express heroism, or love, or anguish. This was the theatricalization of dance; for a dancer who was physically proficient but emotionally lame it provided a dramatic mask, a way of displaying passions that were not sufficiently felt.

Belsky's character class was the perfect complement for Misha's technical skills. Acting class, given by Valentina Osokine, helped still more, although it added hours to a schedule that was already arduous for an adolescent boy. This was a nondance class, another specialty of Russian dance education in which Mikhail was taught how to convey emotions with the simplest of gestures—how to walk sadly, how to stand still anxiously, how to hold the arms in eagerness or anticipation.

The high point of Mikhail's day was his classical ballet class with Alexander Pushkin. This was what he was best at, what he tumbled out of bed for each morning, still fresh and unstressed by the bells that would have him running from one classroom to another all day till he was exhausted. And here it was that he formed his most valuable relationship with a teacher.

Pushkin had seen something he liked in Baryshnikov when the boy had first come to see him during the Latvian Ballet tour, just as he had taken to the young and rebellious Nureyev, Pushkin's previous protégé, when everyone else was ready to expel him because of his overly individualistic attitude. Mikhail Baryshnikov was not like Nureyev, who had been somewhat arrogant, a loner who refused to submit to the Vaganova school's demands for conformity, a passionate young dancer whose technical imperfections were compensated for by sheer expressive impact and raw energy. Nureyev was a romantic.

Misha, on the other hand, was a serious, rather shy boy who was eager to get along with fellow students and with the authorities. His movements were perfect, cool, classical. What the two young dancers shared was a prodigious talent, an intense energy and enthusiasm for dance—each in his own way—and a kind of self-confident ambition to be the best. Both were also alone in Leningrad, both were latecomers and outsiders in a close-knit and sometimes unkind little world, and both were reluctant to become involved in the political circles that were that world's ladder to security and success.

Pushkin had befriended and nurtured and lost Nureyev, and now Baryshnikov came along and Pushkin began to nurture him. Pushkin has been described not only as a brilliant teacher with a brilliant method but also as the kindest and most sensitive of men—"a lovely, loving, careful teacher," the dance critic Clive Barnes has called him. He was "gentle and intelligent," according to Bella Kovarskaya. Says Nureyev, "What he said is still simmering through me." Pushkin had a way of recognizing a dancer's true potential and then helping him discover and develop that potential for himself. It was a process of self-education. In his class of seven boys, Pushkin helped each one excel in an individual, unique way.

Everyone had always thought of Misha as a character dancer. His teachers at Riga and at the Vaganova Institute all thought that his stocky, muscular build, combined with that naive face, would prevent him from succeeding as a *danseur noble*, that he never would be able to play those serious, principal roles like Prince Siegried in *Swan Lake* or Count Albrecht in *Giselle*. A *danseur noble* had to be tall, handsome, and elegantly proportioned with long legs, long muscles, and a noble presence. Instead, Misha was cute. Regardless of his technical abilities, Misha, they felt, would never make it as a principal dancer. He would always be a *demi-caractère* dancer, something short of pure classical. Pushkin was the only one of his teachers who believed that Misha could carry those principal roles. "Just keep going, keep going," he would tell Misha.

Pushkin's classes are now legendary in the world of classical dance, partly because he produced a Nureyev, a Baryshnikov, and several other fine male dancers. It wasn't just the extraordinary relationship he managed to form with his students, or the way he helped them impose discipline from within; it was his method and the structure of his class. Every serious ballet class, anywhere in the world, is divided into two successive parts. The first part is a warm-up, which prepares the muscles for the second part, practicing combinations of steps. If the warm-up period is too short, the muscles must strain to achieve the difficult maneuvers of the second part.

Pushkin's warm-up period was perfect. The timing was perfect, the pacing was perfect, and as Baryshnikov remembers, "then suddenly the pressure starts and the combinations get harder and harder, harder and harder." The second part of the class grew naturally, seamlessly, out of the first, and Pushkin's endlessly varied combinations of steps were such that the dancers had to exert themselves in gradually increasing increments, never straining or jarring, until they had reached the very limits of their capacity. Through Pushkin's method, Misha trained the muscles of his body to work effortlessly, almost automatically, in any combination of steps.

Pushkin's specialty was the grand, acrobatic leap. This had been his hallmark during his own career as a Kirov dancer, and he developed it in Nureyev, Baryshnikov, and another of his students, Yuri Soloviev, who became famous for his leaps. Soloviev seemed to hang in the air, defying gravity. In Nureyev's case it became what Clive Barnes has called a "pantherine leap," a leap of raw grace; Baryshnikov's was more precise, more remote, a sort of soaring in space. But it was Pushkin who developed them all, with an impeccable eye for each dancer's sensibility.

During his three years at the Vaganova, Misha lived in the school dormitory, an austere, brick building on Pravda Street where the children on scholarship—children without family in Leningrad—lived. There he shared a room with about ten other boys. The facilities were meager, the atmosphere institutional; it wasn't much more than a place to sleep between falling into bed exhausted at the end of a long day and being awakened by the duty matron at eight o'clock the next morning. The school itself was more of a home for many of the students, especially for those whose real homes were far away. But Misha never really treated the school like home or his classmates like family. The Vaganova Institute was his place of work. He had friends amongst his fellow students, and he was generally well liked, but he kept an emotional distance. Instead, it was his teacher's home that became his refuge; Pushkin and his wife Kseniia Losifovna Lurgenson, a one-time ballerina, became his parents—just as they had become Nureyev's a few years earlier. Pushkin never spoke about Nureyev. Once, Misha found a photograph of the dancer in Pushkin's apartment and asked who it was. That was the first he heard about the great defector.

As time went by, Misha became more and more a part of Pushkin's life. He would go to his house when school was over, alone or with one or two other students. Kseniia would cook some good, simple food and they would eat together. The Push-kins epitomized Leningrad's tradition of hospitality; the boys were always hungry, and here was an ever-welcoming kitchen. It was a warm, relaxing home. Classical records were played and there were books to read and interesting discussions to follow— discussions about music, art, literature, movies, and dance. Misha felt welcome and comfortable in the close, cultured atmo-sphere of the Pushkins' tiny apartment.

Sometimes, friends of the Pushkins would come by, mostly artists or musicians and teachers from the university, people in their twenties and thirties. Misha enjoyed their company. Their interests were broad and sophisticated, and for Misha, who was growing up fast, they represented an adult world far more attrac-tive than the isolated one of the ballet school.

Misha listened intently to everything that was said, and he spoke very little. He was always learning. He aspired not only to the intellectualism but also to the manners that he observed in these cultivated Leningraders. They were the heirs to Peter the Great's vision of Leningrad as the bridge to the West. Peter had promoted industrialization and science, but he also had ordered courtiers to wear European clothes and noblewomen to appear publicly in the latest German fashions. In their speech, their dress, and their hospitality, Pushkin and his friends displayed an inherent nobility that Misha liked and respected enormously. Anxious to become one of them, he quickly learned to speak the "good Russian" of Leningrad, leaving behind him the provincial Russian with which he had grown up in Latvia. "Respect for language is respect for yourself," Misha once said. "It lifts you up." Already he knew that to grow as a dancer he had to grow as a person.

Often Pushkin would suggest some after-dinner dance exercises, and Misha would do his forty-five minutes at the barre and twenty jumps while his teacher took a stroll among the elegant crowds on Nevsky Prospekt. Then it would be too late for Misha to return to the dormitory, so he would sleep at the Pushkins' and go straight from there to school in the morning.

Mikhail Baryshnikov thrived under Pushkin's loving guidance. He knew he was doing well in dance—that he could dance anything and make it look easy—so he stopped worrying so much. He was becoming more self-assured, even though he still hated to be called cute and still wished he could look tough and "bad," like a "cool kind of guy." Misha wasn't one of the cool guys, but he was starting to gain a reputation as a prodigy, a phenomenon, and Pushkin's favorite student. Dancers at the Kirov began to talk about his incredible abilities and his "unfortunate" looks. The dancers told some critics, and one or two of the critics went to see for themselves. Watching from the balcony overlooking the large studio as Pushkin's class worked down below, the critic Gennady Shmakov noticed something very special about the "frail looking, fair boy with distant, luminous eyes and sharp features."

In early 1966, at age seventeen, Baryshnikov was sent to Bulgaria to compete in the international ballet competition at Varna, a resort town. It was his first time outside the Soviet Union and it was hot, nerve-racking, and crammed with visitors from all over the world. Natalia Makarova of the Kirov Ballet had come home from Varna the previous year with the cherished gold medal, to great acclaim. Misha was eight years her junior and still a student, but he, too, returned to Leningrad with the gold medal—one of the most important ballet prizes an individual dancer can win. Of course, neither Makarova nor Baryshnikov could have guessed that within ten years their names, as defectors, would have been erased from the Varna roll of honor.

Misha's final, graduating year had begun, and tensions were rising. The fifteen or so students who would be finishing their studies and leaving the hard but safe, protected world of the Vaganova Institute began to think seriously about what lay ahead. Only two or three would be ceremoniously accepted into the illustrious Kirov Ballet; the losers would have to accept positions in the obscure provincial ballet companies, isolated from the beauty and history of the big city that had become their home.

Misha was pretty confident about his own future, yet even for him this final year wasn't easy. Exams in the academic subjects loomed ominously, and dance class discipline intensified in preparation for the final exam, which was rigidly designed to judge technical proficiency. As the students worked to perfect their steps, jealousies emerged and political maneuvering escalated. Misha kept his distance from the intrigues that developed. He knew he was a dancer, pure and simple; that in itself was his strength. He knew he didn't have to find favor with the authorities by involving himself in party activities; besides, he had no interest in politics and resented its intrusion into the world of dance. On the other hand, he kept such opinions to himself. Students and full-fledged dancers alike were expected to conform to the collective spirit. During his three years at Vaganova, Misha had neither said nor done anything to draw attention to himself, except dance. He couldn't be faulted on the grounds of either excessive individualism or excessive independence of thought.

Adding to the pressures of the final year, senior students were required to give regular recitals in the school's two-hundred-seat theater, where they were watched from the front rows by hawk-eyed teachers and various ballet company representatives and from the overcrowded back rows by awestruck boys and girls of the younger classes. The children "roared so after each number," recalls Valery Panov in his autobiography, "that the front of the house had to restrain them before the curtain could rise again." Pushkin would be there, of course, taking mental notes, ready to make some correction when it was all over. Meanwhile, in the classrooms near the theater, nervous senior students applied their stage makeup between the rows of desks and waited for the terrible thrill of being summoned for their individual performances.

Ice melted on the Neva River, making tinkling sounds as it cracked, snow turned to gray slush, and the days grew longer and brighter as the hard Leningrad winter turned to spring. The exams came and went. Misha found himself on the brink of the future the whole class had hoped for and must have known Baryshnikov would win: a place with the Kirov Ballet. It was inevitable. In Mikhail Baryshnikov the promise of the Vaganova Institute was fulfilled; the school would provide the theater with a dancer trained to fit precisely into the Kirov mold, a dancer who had mastered the rigid discipline of classical ballet to the point of exquisite perfection.

The white nights of Leningrad drew near, those legendary, luminous nights called the "poetry of God" by Dumas, when the sun barely sets in the northern skies and the city, all golds and grays and pastels, abandons itself to romance. A white night is hushed, ethereal, timeless. Even by day there is a strange energy in the air. Few people are untouched by the magic of these three weeks. Dark moods lift; lovers stroll along the canals; dormitory doors stay open late; the police relax and look away. The city has lived all year for this brief season. The White Nights Festival is a mardi gras of the northern latitudes and, like mardi gras, is given over to song and dance—Russian style. During this four-day festival of the arts, hordes of tourists join Leningraders for a feast of theater, music, ballet, and opera. Outdoor stages are erected in the parks, and stars make guest appearances in the city's theaters. For ballet lovers, the high point of the festival is the evening of Vaganova pregraduation recitals on the Kirov stage. As the days lengthened, Misha set about preparing for his performance.

SIX

A Legend in
the Making

THE EVENING OF recitals marked an end and
a beginning in an otherwise unbroken succession
of days and years devoted to being a dancer.
Things wouldn't change much in the course of his career—the
grinding discipline of daily class would continue; the long,
sometimes lonely hours of practice needed just to keep the muscles tuned; the responsibilities to dance as an almost sacred profession; the rehearsals; and the thrill of the stage. On the other
hand, some things in life would be different. There would be no
more math or history or any other academic classes. Misha
would be a professional dancer. He would be paid, he would be
given an apartment, and, if he was lucky, there would be tours
abroad. Besides, there would be the glory of belonging to the
great Kirov Ballet, the second-oldest ballet company in the
world. For if the Kirov is the nation's citadel of ideal beauty, its
members are the shining knights who protect for their nation's
masses the possibility of effortless grace.

The evening graduation recitals at the Kirov were an old

Leningrad tradition. This was one of the most eagerly antici-
pated events of the ballet year, both for the students and for the
fans. Tickets would sell out months in advance. Each year the
theater practically overflowed with tourists, ballet fans, and rela-
tives and friends of the graduating students. Teachers and critics,
who came to evaluate the new generation of dancers, filled the
best seats.

Meanwhile, the students stood in the wings, nerves taut. It
was a serious occasion, four hours of predominantly dutiful pas
de deux and variations repeated year after year, so that the audience by now knew every step, every deviation. While the
tourists would applaud at every curtain, the fans and critics
would soon become jaded by the whole affair. They seemed to
derive more pleasure from the occasional flawed performance, to
which they could respond with their terrible silence, than from
the many adequate displays that demanded their polite applause.
They would count *fouettés*, just in case the student did thirty-
three in a row instead of thirty-two, and they could instantly
recognize original technique when they saw it. The entertainment lay not in novelty but in comparing this year's talents with
those of last year and the previous year. Perhaps there would be
a budding star. Nureyev had danced here on this same evening
only a few years before, and Nijinsky had been discovered here
over half a century earlier.

Baryshnikov's performance on that white night of 1966 was
the stuff of legend. Certainly, it was not the first time that the
audience had seen the variation from *Le Corsaire*. It was one of the
"approved" pieces so often danced by students and Kirov members whenever they needed a classic that would allow them to
show off their technical abilities. The ballet had been in the
Kirov repertoire since its Imperial days, when the spectacle of
stormy seas was created by a detachment of the czar's guards,
who would lie under the ocean dropcloth and heave. This year,
halfway through the evening, the entire audience woke up and

took notice as young Mikhail Baryshnikov came on stage and began to dance.

He stepped onto the stage in his bright green harem pants, a brilliant wide belt around his waist, a silver-plumed headband circling his forehead, his torso bare and boyish. He was a touchingly young slave. Almost without preparation, he embarked on a miraculous, effortless series of turns and leaps punctuated by a perfect, whirling grand pirouette that left the audience breathless. Nureyev's graduate performance of the same piece had overflowed with an electric sensuality. Baryshnikov's slave was joyful, exuberant, charmingly light as air. It had been a long time since the Kirov had seen such perfection, such unaffected virtuosity. "Baryshnikov created the rare impression of a body dancing by itself, without instructions," wrote critic Gennady Shmakov. Never had he seen anything like it. But some of the older fans remembered Nijinsky's legendary leap in his first Kirov performance of *Blue Bird* on November 7, 1907, and they immediately made the connection with Baryshnikov. No, Baryshnikov was not another Nureyev, he was more a Nijinsky, the great Nijinsky who had danced himself to madness.

Misha's performance nearly brought down the house. "The cries of 'Bravo' seemed to shake the painted vaults of the theater, threatening to fell the chandeliers and crack the layers of gilding," recalls Shmakov. If a second revolution had been erupting outside, not a soul in that theater would have realized it. Later, as the curtain fell and the crowds left the lavish baroque auditorium to exchange comments in the lobby, the name Baryshnikov was on every tongue. How he had danced! What purity of style! And what youthful charm! As he stood in the lobby that evening, Shmakov heard Nijinsky's name being evoked in the same breath as that of the eighteen-year-old dancer who had just captured the imagination of Leningrad. He asked the venerable former prima ballerina Elizaveta Time whether Baryshnikov's performance had reminded her of Nijinsky. "Nijinsky never danced like that," she told Shmakov, "and did not possess such devastating charm. . . . No one in my memory danced the way this boy dances."

Soon it was the end of the term on Rossi Street, a solemn occasion for the graduating students. Diplomas were presented, students and teachers shook hands, speeches were dutifully made, and the party, school, and students were toasted—with half-full glasses of wine, befitting the Vaganova school's monastic discipline. When it was all over, the graduates promenaded down the center of the elegant Nevsky Prospekt toward the Winter Palace. It was a tradition, like so many other things in the life of a Russian dancer; it was the Vaganova way of celebrating the liberation from school, the end of an era. Then came contemplation of the future and, for some, nostalgia or excitement. There would be a parting of the ways. Some would remain in Leningrad, but most would have to leave.

Baryshnikov was staying. Moreover, in a rare waiver of the Kirov's rigid hierarchical scheme, he was to be propelled directly to soloist rank. Throughout the world, and especially in Russia, ballet dancers are required to develop for several years in the relative obscurity of the corps de ballet before being entrusted with solo or leading roles. Only a very few dancers in the long history of the Kirov have jumped the ladder of promotion from the corps to soloist. Already Misha was following in the legendary footsteps of Nijinsky, Nureyev, and Pavlova.

Misha was a natural heir to the Kirov tradition. The Kirov Ballet is not as well known in the West as Moscow's Bolshoi Ballet. Yet in Russia, as well as in Western ballet circles, the Kirov has long been considered the true home of classical ballet, and its dancers have been known as the most perfectly trained classicists in the world. The Bolshoi is like the city it inhabits: important, expansive, vital, a hodgepodge of styles, spectacular. It has to please the often unsophisticated Moscow politicians who frequent it. The Kirov, on the other hand, belongs to Leningrad. Its standards are more austere than those of the

Bolshoi. It is less showy, more stylized, and devotedly elegant and historic. It appeals to the refined tastes cultivated by its Leningrad audience. The Bolshoi enjoys more funding and more travel, but the Kirov receives more critical acclaim.

The Kirov has its roots in the opera and ballet company founded at the Bolshoi Theatre in St. Petersburg in 1738. In 1860, performances began at the Maryinsky Theatre. St. Petersburg at that time was the fashionable capital of Russia. The ballet was in the service of the czars and the aristocracy. Orders and privileges came directly from the court. If a moody prince disliked the color of the ballerina's tutu or was displeased by a new piece of choreography, that would all be put right before the next performance. After the Revolution this system of patronage was continued, except that dancers now performed for the state. The many ballet companies of the Soviet Union are lavishly supported and controlled by the Communist party, under the auspices of the Ministry of Culture. In Russia, ballet dancers have never gone hungry or in rags.

As a professional ballet dancer, Misha became a civil servant. Above him the chain of command extended from the theater's artistic director all the way to Moscow's central party leadership. Like most civil service positions, it was a comfortable job. He was given a salary of two hundred dollars a month—more than a skilled worker with a family would make—and was provided with a place to live. He was entitled to three months of summer vacation a year, one month's leave for sickness or injury, health care, and a pension. And he could relax in the knowledge that he never would be overworked.

From the time he gave his first interviews after defecting to the West Misha spoke effusively about the Kirov Ballet. He said time and time again that he loved his old theater and missed it terribly. Not everyone believed him then. After all, he had fled. But in fact, from the very beginning the Kirov had a hold on Misha, and it always would. Even after his teenage illusions had been shattered, Misha held onto an image of his ideal Kirov, repository of the greatest and purest ballet tradition in the world.

Misha missed the Kirov because it was his home. He didn't have another. When he joined the company he was eighteen, and although he had been visiting his father in Riga during summer vacations, Riga wasn't home. The apartment he had been allocated by the theater was communal, shared with a family. He couldn't make a home for himself there; like the student dormitory, it was a place to sleep. He still had a surrogate father in Pushkin, whose *classe de excellence* at the Vaganova he continued to take once a day. But the theater represented Misha's base, his caretaker, authority figure, and provider. He was dependent on it. Like ballet companies everywhere it was a unique, narrow community, and it was almost all that Misha knew of the world.

Yet it wasn't only because it was home that Misha clung nostalgically to his image of the Kirov. Anyone who had spent time in the museum on the fifth floor of the Vaganova Institute knew that Leningrad's Kirov was the birthplace and cradle of Russian ballet. This was where the two great nineteenth-century French ballet masters Charles Didelot and Marius Petipa had come, and here they had superimposed the courtly traditions of French ballet with the dramatic folk dances, the acrobatics, and the passion for spectacle and drama of the Russian people. With this fusion, and in this theater, Russia had made ballet its own, and the Kirov Theater became the center of classical ballet worldwide. Here Petipa had choreographed the great story ballets of Tchaikovsky that we now associate with Russian dance—*Sleeping Beauty*, *Nutcracker*, and *Swan Lake*.

When he danced on the Kirov stage Misha became a part of this great tradition. The theater dated from Petipa's days, and many still prefer the ring of its original name, the Maryinsky. It was renamed the State Academic Theater for Opera and Ballet following the Revolution, and under Stalin it became the Kirov Theater, after Sergei Kirov, the Leningrad party chief who, ironically, was later shot as a first step in Stalin's reign of terror.

Besides its name, little had changed at the old Maryinsky between the era of Petipa and the czars and Misha's days as a Kirov dancer.

By the end of World War II, with Leningrad cold, hungry, and shattered after its three-year siege, the Kirov was so important to life in the city that top priority was given to its reconstruction. Six-hundred-and-fifty-thousand people had died of starvation, and many were still starving. Whole streets had been demolished by shells. But within days of the war's end, two hundred men from the Red Army were at work inside the once-glittering Kirov, restoring every detail of its imperial splendor, from the heating system to the plush stalls and the crystal. "If we can't open on May 1st I don't know what the people will say," the director of repairs told an English journalist, Iris Morley. "It makes us feel when the theater is open that life has begun again." The Kirov was, and remains, a hallowed place, a place, as Morley wrote then, "where the impulses of every shabby hungry factory worker for poetry [and] magnificence in living" could find an outlet.

The theater that Misha became a part of in 1967 was almost exactly the same theater in which the czars and czarinas had dispensed favors from the plush Imperial box a century earlier. It was a small yet grand auditorium, ornately carved and elegantly proportioned, a gem of gold and azure. Every detail had been preserved or restored. Even the curtain remained—a huge swag of blue velvet lavishly embroidered in gold thread. Only the Imperial insignia over the former Imperial box was absent, replaced by the hammer-and-sickle emblem of the Soviet Union. In every other way this most exquisite of theaters remained the same—despite a massive revolution, two world wars, and a terrible siege of the city. It was a wonderful place to dance. No matter where in the world Misha performed later in his life, only once or twice did he find a theater that inspired him as did the old Maryinsky.

During those early years in the West, when Misha yearned to

dance again on the Kirov stage, he remembered and longed for his audience there, too. Never again would he dance for an audience that was so committed, informed, and passionate about dance. Ballet is to the Russian people, including the ordinary working people, what baseball is to Americans: an irreplaceable part of national life, complete with the most loyal of fans. In the earliest days of Russian ballet the fans were aristocrats. Around their necks they wore small cards printed with the names of their favorite dancers. Even Stalin was a fan; he fell for a Kirov ballerina and spared the aristocratic art of ballet, although in a far less aristocratic form. The first Bolshevik commissar of education, Anatole Lunacharsky, was a ballet fan, too. It was he who persuaded the revolutionary authorities to reopen the Maryinsky Theatre and its school after a brief closing during the hard winter of 1917. Lunacharsky knew that ballet was as important for Russia as her pig-iron factories.

He was proved right. When the state reopened the theater after the Revolution it was hardly a budgetary priority. The boys at the ballet school made shirts for themselves out of the theater's velvet draperies. There was no heat in the theater, and the dancers could see their breath in the icy air. Members of the audience peered from under blankets, stamping their feet to keep warm. Yet the people came in droves to see the ballet.

Despite their cherished status among the Russian people, ballet dancers like Misha had to endure the same poor living standards as the average worker. Even a leading dancer was scarcely better off than a skilled carpenter. Misha's room in the communal apartment was on the first floor of a bleak, modern building on dingy Kolpinskaya Street, across the Neva on the Petrograd side, where many university people lived. When he looked out his one window he saw only the garbage piled on the street corner. His room was bare, almost unfurnished. Furniture was expensive, and Misha was poor. But he was only nineteen years old and had a room to himself, so he was better off than many his age.

As a Kirov soloist Misha was better paid and had more privileges than dancers in any other Soviet company except the Bolshoi. The Kirov was fully equipped to take special care of its two-hundred dancers. There were ultramodern workshops turning out lavish sets, props, and special effects; a large catering department; a crowd of assistant directors who attended the wings whenever there were dancers performing; makeup men, costumers, wardrobe mistresses, doctors, dentists, physiotherapists, and surgeons, all at the service of the Kirov dancers.

For a while Misha was happy dancing for the state. He had plenty of time to read new books, see new movies, and attend new productions at any of the theaters in Leningrad and, when he could, in Moscow. He became a voracious culturephile, gobbling up anything that might expand him. He needed information like a tree needs water. For a ballet dancer he was abnormally curious about the world outside the Kirov. He continued to make new friends among the Leningrad intelligentsia, attaching himself gradually to couples and families with warm homes and questioning minds. He needed the stability as much as he wanted the stimulation.

As time went by, Misha began to turn up at his friends' homes with a tall, slender girl called Tanya. It had taken him some time to win her over. Tatyana Koltsova, or Tanya as friends called her, was a senior Vaganova student when Misha first took a liking to her. Misha was in his first year with the Kirov, yet already his name had achieved giant proportions around the school, where he still went for rehearsals and coaching sessions—and to peek at classes of up-and-coming ballerinas. Like a few other Kirov "stage bachelors," Misha was on the lookout for a perfect dance partner. Obviously on his way to becoming a star, he could have his pick of the corps de ballet. Scarcely a dancer yet, Tanya was a little intimidated by Misha. For a while she avoided his advances, while he tried to win her trust and convince her that he was just a regular guy. So began an on again, off again relationship that would continue through Misha's first years at the Kirov.

In the beginning Misha's unusual status gave him problems in the professional class for Kirov dancers that he took with Pushkin. While on the whole his playfulness made him popular among fellow dancers, some of the more established male soloists in the class were jealous of this talented young newcomer. Since they couldn't find fault with his technique, they made fun of his physique, which for their purposes deviated just enough from the Kirov norm. The fact was, Baryshnikov was different, and in the strictly disciplined atmosphere of the Kirov, differences were hard to tolerate. Behind his back they called him a "hockey puck" and complained that he "darted around" so fast that they couldn't keep up with him. They accused him of being all technique, no soul. In lift classes, designed to develop partnering skills, they noted how his young body wobbled under a partner's weight. Misha's arms and chest were still weak, but his muscles would develop with practice and age. The men who teased him would never progress further than their present level, and they knew it. As Misha began to prove himself on stage, the teasing stopped.

Soon after Misha joined the class, the critic Clive Barnes came to Leningrad and spent some time observing Pushkin at work. In particular, he noticed an unusual amount of attention being given to one strangely serious-looking young man, "18 or 19, fair haired, cherubic, and the most perfect dancer I have ever seen. I asked his name. It was Yuri Baryshnikov." "Yuri" was Misha, and through Barnes, news of Baryshnikov's virtuosity reached the West for the first time. A few Russian critics were singing his praises, too, despite the fact that Misha had scarcely been given an opportunity to develop on the Kirov stage.

For a while Baryshnikov dutifully danced in the kinds of roles for which he was considered best suited. He danced the classical showpieces in concert programs, mainly pas de deux that showed off his technical virtuosity without really challenging him. And he danced solo roles in the social-realist ballets that were so popular with the party elite. Much to his disappointment, Misha was seen as the perfect heroic Soviet youth, the ultimate cosmonaut, the noble worker. The great, classical male roles that he longed to tackle were reserved for older dancers with nobler features—the tall and handsome types. With his puppyish qualities nobody could imagine Misha as a prince. At the same time, there was a dearth of modern ballets available in which Misha might have learned new ideas and new ways of moving. Nevertheless, Misha was patient. He had time, and there was always something to be learned, no matter what the role. Pushkin was watching over him, following his performances on the Kirov stage, and giving him all the instruction and advice he needed.

In June 1969 the Kirov entered Baryshnikov in the first International Ballet Competition in Moscow. The competition, open to dancers aged eighteen to twenty-eight, was a huge event. Twenty judges from fourteen countries watched for a week while twenty-six dancers from eighteen countries performed their set pieces on the Bolshoi stage to piano accompaniment. The judges were presided over by the immortal Russian ballerina, Galina Ulanova, and included the American Agnes de Mille, the Russian composer Aram Khachaturian, and various critics, theater directors, dancers, and choreographers. The legendary Serge Lifar, who had left Russia during the Revolution to work with Diaghilev, was there as an honored guest, and the theater was crammed with representatives of the Soviet government, foreign diplomats, reporters from all over the world, and Soviet dancers eager to catch a glimpse of international ballet. Outside the theater people scrambled and begged for tickets. Reports of the competition made front-page news in the Moscow dailies.

Western visitors were amazed at the scene. After all, these dancers weren't stars, they were young and largely unknown. Yet the adoration was lavish. It is no wonder, thought Agnes de

Mille, that the young Soviets perform their athletic stunts so happily. "When a Soviet soloist takes the stage he can do what is almost not possible to do, and with an exuberance, childish in its purity and unalloyed joy, that comes when one knows that one is essential. The whole world recognizes this quality."

De Mille might have been talking about Baryshnikov. He performed a short, contemporary ballet, *Vestris*, which had been choreographed for him for the occasion by Leonid Yacobson, an inspired and irreverent choreographer who had a way of tapping the dancer's individuality and shocking the Kirov's conservative bastions. Working with Yacobson was a revelation for Misha, for he was introduced to a kind of modern, grotesque dancing that was completely new to him and completely fascinating. What fascinated everyone else, however, was the revelation that Misha was not only a technical genius but a talented mime as well.

Based on the life of Auguste Vestris, a legendary dancer, *Vestris* is a historical biography in seven chapters, each lasting one minute and each requiring a drastic change in style and personality. This was the first role created specifically for Baryshnikov, and it was the first time that anyone had recognized his incredible capacity for self-transformation. Yacobson saw how Misha liked to fool around, clowning and impersonating everybody from James Cagney to Konstantin Sergeyev, the Kirov's artistic director. He recognized the comic in him and produced a ballet that fused a whole range of technical challenges with a lot of pantomime.

Misha won the gold prize for soloists and high praise from Maya Plisetskaya, who gave him thirteen out of twelve points. Helgi Tomasson of the United States won a silver and two French dancers won the gold for partners in a highly controversial, erotic ballet by the fashionable choreographer Maurice Béjart. It was Béjart's daring ballet, not the joyous feats of Misha and the Soviets, that brought the house down, causing a great deal of consternation among the Soviet establishment. Misha went home to Leningrad with his medal and was rewarded with a small salary raise. The Kirov establishment was proud of him, but they hated Yacobson's ballet. Baryshnikov was now twenty and on the verge of a series of successes that would secure his place as a leading dancer and leave him longing for more. For the more successful Misha became, the more he felt constrained by the narrow world of the Kirov and the more he longed to dance in precisely the kind of works that were so controversial in the Soviet Union.

SEVEN

Albrecht and Giselle

IN 1969 BARYSHNIKOV won the Moscow international prize and the Nijinsky prize of Paris. In November of that year he made his debut in his first leading role, as Basil in *Don Quixote*. He was technically astounding. The public loved him. He made *Don Quixote* a huge success for the Kirov, so the Kirov loved him, too. Immediately Misha was recognized as the best Basil in Leningrad, perhaps even the best dancer in Leningrad. His technique was breathtaking. He seemed to be chasing an ideal. Emotionally his dancing was cool and cerebral, as if perfection were a mask.

Misha was happy and excited. Success felt good. And there was yet another challenge in the works: one of the Kirov's leading dancers and most rebellious choreographers, Igor Tchernichov had been staging a new, one-act *Romeo and Juliet* with Kirov dancers Natalia Makarova and Vadim Gulyaev as the star-crossed lovers and Valery Panov as Tybalt. When Misha came to Tchernichov's attention he decided to expand his work to include the role of Mercutio, Romeo's playful, irreverent young

52

friend. Misha, thought Tchernichov, would make the perfect Mercutio.

It was around this time that Misha reportedly fell in love with Natalia Makarova. He was twenty-one, she was almost thirty, a small, delicate woman who was much more sophisticated than Tatyana Koltsova. Baryshnikov was infatuated with Makarova. He would do anything for her. Her marriage had recently fallen apart and she was bitter; the Kirov had begun to feel like a trap filled with serpents. But Misha was different. To Makarova, he was just a boy. He was Mercutio. His freshness was attractive to her, and his innocence and sincerity were like a pocket of pure air in the middle of smog. Misha was alive, exuberant. And he danced like an angel.

Natalia Makarova was one of the Kirov's most exquisitely intuitive ballerinas. She danced everything her own way. She decided night by night how she felt in her role, and she played it spontaneously. Makarova had graduated from the Vaganova Institute in 1958, and by now she had no illusions left about the Kirov. She had never been allowed to expand. She had never had the opportunity to dance in a role that really suited her, and no roles had been created for her. Unlike Irina Kolpakova, who as an active party member managed to get what she wanted in the theater much of the time, Makarova avoided any involvement in party politics by acting the part of the dumb blonde. Except when she danced. Tchernichov's *Romeo and Juliet* was one of the best things that had happened to her in her Kirov career.

Since the production wasn't part of the Kirov's scheduled season, the participants worked on it without pay and had to schedule rehearsals to fit into their already loaded workdays. Makarova, Panov, and Baryshnikov rehearsed for six months. At the final dress rehearsals an audience consisting of approved critics and representatives from the Ministry of Culture and from the Kirov Theater came to preview the work. This was standard practice for every new production. If changes were required, they could be made in time for the public debut.

The audience watched the preview of *Romeo and Juliet* in horrified silence, and the ballet was banned on the spot. It was considered decadent. It was erotic, immoral, and formal. The arabesques, said Konstantin Sergeyev, were Western arabesques, not Soviet arabesques. "This flower of evil must never be permitted to blossom," Maria-Marietta Frangopolo proclaimed. It was a terrible blow for everyone involved. Later, Irina Kolpakova persuaded the authorities to let her stage the ballet once as part of a personal "creative evening," with herself in the role of Juliet. Makarova never danced the role in the Soviet Union; Panov and Baryshnikov never danced in the ballet again; and Tchernichov was eventually sent to the provinces.

Unfortunately, Misha had joined the Kirov at a particularly stagnant period in its history. For all its lavish state funding, its impeccable coaching, and its golden tradition, the Kirov was in a sad, muddled state by the end of the 1960s. Here was a theater that could afford to spend an entire year staging a new ballet—a luxury by Western standards—yet its repertoire was frozen in the safety of the past.

It wasn't only the Kirov that was stagnant and riddled with party bureaucracy, it was the country in general. The Soviet Union had just invaded Czechoslovakia. The need for ideological correctness was being reaffirmed in every area after the liberalizations of the Khrushchev years. In the shake-up following Nureyev's defection the Kirov post of administrative director had been given to a hardliner named Petr Rachinsky—also known as "the fireman," after his previous occupation. His job was to protect the people from decadent ideas and deviant forms. The few established Kirov choreographers with inventive ideas had been more or less put out to pasture by the pious Sergeyev, Western ballets were strictly off-limits, and Russian ballet, at least, as Leningrad knew it, was coming to depend almost entirely on technical superlatives. The athletic qualities of ballet that had been promoted after the Revolution as a way of relating to the common people had by now almost entirely replaced artistic innovation.

Misha had been happy to dance for the state, happy to be part of such a prestigious and perfected tradition. But the more he danced, the more successful he became, the more he felt constrained by the lack of creative opportunities open to him.

It was December in Leningrad—damp, raw, and muffled by snow. The city grew dark by three o'clock every afternoon and stayed dark until nine or ten in the morning. Temperatures never rose above zero. A long winter lay ahead. *Romeo and Juliet* was a nonballet, and Misha was beginning to understand the political dynamics of the Kirov. There were rumors of a foreign tour; several dancers would be chosen to perform in London and Holland, and everyone wanted to go. Foreign tours were highly desirable to Soviet dancers because they provided an opportunity to be noticed in the West and to earn foreign currency with which the dancers could buy luxury items like television sets, stereos, jeans, and lingerie, which were available only in foreign currency stores—*beriozky*—or on the black market. Since dancers were picked on the basis of "correct" attitudes, the pressure to conform intensified before each foreign tour. KGB informants within the company watched suspect dancers and reported back to the personnel department. Any dancer who might pose a so-called security risk simply stayed home.

Such had been the plight of Valery Panov, who in 1959 was suddenly sent back from New York mid-tour because he showed too much interest in American life-styles. Panov hadn't toured the West since then. Nureyev defected in Paris in 1961 because he guessed that the same treatment was in store for him. It helped to be a party member, which demonstrated one's loyalty and stability. Dancers could also help themselves by exposing other dancers' incorrect attitudes. Since the tour lists were kept officially secret until it was almost time to leave, the backbiting and the tension could become almost unbearable.

In March 1970 a piece of Misha's world suddenly slipped away. Alexander Pushkin collapsed on the street with a heart attack and died. He was sixty-two. Pushkin's death marked the end of an era for both Misha and Russian ballet. He was the last of the legendary teachers. Nobody could replace him. Suddenly, Misha had lost a father figure, a dedicated teacher, and a valuable ally. He was heartbroken. "I realized that I was totally on my own."

Every great dancer has given credit to the teacher who made it possible. Ballet is an intangible tradition handed down from generation to generation—there's no other way it can be learned. Now Misha felt it was his turn. As a tribute to Pushkin and the tradition he had preserved, Misha took over his teacher's Vaganova class of senior boys, who were nearing their final exams. He was twenty-two; his students were seventeen.

Misha had no interest in the political intrigues of the Kirov and was too inexperienced and idealistic to take all of it in stride. Alienated, he kept his distance, kept his mouth shut, immersed himself in work, and hoped to be picked for his talents. He didn't dare to express his opinions to anyone because he never knew whom he could trust. Sometimes he wasn't even sure about his opinions; without Pushkin's guidance it became even harder for Misha to know what was good and what was bad. Occasionally he felt forced to compromise—especially when there was a tour coming up. How else could he get ahead?

Sergeyev was at this time staging a production of *Hamlet*, with Natalia Makarova as Ophelia and Baryshnikov as the young prince. The role of Hamlet could have been perfect for Misha. However, it soon became obvious that this was another of the artistic director's bland attempts at choreography, although nobody said so publicly, and that Hamlet was developing into just another exercise in technical wizardry. Misha was embarrassed by his role. Nevertheless, he said nothing and just kept on rehearsing.

When the time came, Baryshnikov and Makarova were both

on the list for the Kirov tour of London and Holland, scheduled
for the late summer of 1970. This was to be Misha's first tour in
the West, his first chance to see and experience a part of the
world that had been under lock and key. The company flew into
London in August and the dancers were taken directly to their
hotels. As Makarova got out of the car Baryshnikov said, "So
don't disappear." Would he follow her if she did? asked
Makarova. "To the ends of the earth," Baryshnikov replied. But
Makarova had no plans to disappear. Actually, the tour leaders
were more worried about Misha, who was beginning to show an
unhealthy liking for Western girls, blue jeans, and modern
ballet.

Misha was curious. He spent every moment of his free time
exploring the cultural offerings of the West. He saw *Fiddler on the
Roof* and *Jesus Christ Superstar* as well as movies like *West Side Story*.
He bought his first Simon and Garfunkel album to add to his
collection of classical music and songsters like Jacques Brel and
Charles Aznavour. He saw the Royal Ballet and American Ballet
Theatre, which happened to be performing at Covent Garden.
And he saw modern dance companies like London's Contempo-
rary Dance Theater: "It was a shocking experience."

Misha was curious, and he was reckless, too. While in
London he met Christina Berlin, daughter of retired Hearst executive Richard Berlin. Tina had been a ballet fan ever since she
could remember; as a girl she had saved her allowance to buy
flowers for her favorite dancers. Now she was working in
London as personal assistant to Margot Fonteyn. She was known
as a socialite, but in fact, she was a rather shy and intense young
woman who fell obsessively in love with Misha. A tenuous romance developed between the two in London. A few months
later Christina visited Leningrad for a week in order to see him.
But Misha had learned to be careful. The theater had tightened
its security; if he wanted to tour, he had to be wary of any
involvement with westerners. Besides, by then his relationship
with Tanya Koltsova was settling down into something serious.

Berlin returned to New York, took a Berlitz course in Russian, dated a Russian journalist, and wrote letters to Misha in Leningrad. The letters were returned unopened.

But in London Misha did take risks. He even slipped away to see Rudolf Nureyev, who had sent a message asking to see Misha. He arranged for Misha to be smuggled in a car to his house one morning, and there they spent the day together talking about ballet, about Pushkin and his wife, and about Leningrad. Nureyev was thirsting for information about the life he had left behind almost ten years earlier, and Baryshnikov was full of curiosity about the nature of ballet in the West. Nureyev didn't talk about his defection, and Baryshnikov didn't ask. He only had to look. Nureyev was surrounded by beautiful possessions; the house where he brought Baryshnikov was lovely. He could have almost anything he wanted, and he was free to dance where and how he wanted. Yet Misha claims that it never crossed his mind to follow in Nureyev's footsteps. He was only just becoming a man, and he had plenty to think about at home in Leningrad.

London was Misha's first taste of a world fundamentally different than the one he was used to. The Kirov was there for a month and he was so busy dancing and looking that he scarcely had time to think about what he was experiencing. Everything was happening so fast. He was showered with attention. The British loved him. Although he was the youngest principal in the company, he electrified his audiences, who compared him to another Kirov dancer they loved so much, Yuri Soloviev. It was a revelation to Misha to realize that he could be a success not just in Leningrad but in London, too. "Well, they're not such barbarians after all," he thought to himself.

At the end of the final performance, as the crowds stood and cheered, Misha was pushed to the front of the stage to take a solitary bow. A critic in the audience, Patricia Barnes, later wrote that she never would forget the sight of Misha as he stood on the flower-strewn stage, the line of illustrious Kirov dancers stretched across the stage behind him. He looked "very young, overawed and vulnerable." Makarova wasn't there that night. All of a sudden, near the end of the tour, she had defected. Nobody had expected it, least of all Makarova herself. Misha was astounded, hurt, a little confused. Sergeyev was miserable. His Ophelia had gone mad, he said. Everyone was surprised. They had been expecting it to be Baryshnikov, not Makarova.

As Makarova tells it, her defection was a split-second, cut-and-dry decision. She'd bought a car in London and made arrangements to have it shipped to Leningrad, so she certainly had not been planning to stay. Yet she didn't surprise herself when, during dinner with friends, she did decide to defect. Suddenly, at the mere suggestion of her dinner host, she decided, cried bitterly for fifteen minutes, and then said she was ready, please call the police. She never went back to the hotel.

The Kirov cancelled its friendship banquets, finished the tour, and returned to a dreary Leningrad fall. The wind that blew in from the Gulf of Finland was damp and bitter. The city was lost in fog, swamped by mud from the endless rains. As work began for the start of a new Kirov season, the company waited for the big shake-up—the kind of upheaval that had followed Nureyev's defection. There were the inevitable letters to Makarova, alternately imploring and chastising, from Sergeyev and a few fellow ballerinas. Controls were tightened. The dancers created their own safety net by damning Makarova publicly as either a traitor or an idiot; Misha quite sincerely believed that she had committed the most stupid act of her life. As for Sergeyev, he was slowly frozen out, undermined and ostracized over a period of several months until his grip on power had crumbled. Rachinsky stayed on as administrative director, although some time later he was quietly dismissed over an embezzlement charge.

The freeze on Sergeyev, which apparently was devised by party-faithful Irina Kolpakova, centered on his production of *Hamlet*, and like most Kirov intrigues, it was played out at regular company meetings. The peer pressure was enormous. Suddenly, word went out that *Hamlet* was a "sorry farce" bound for disaster. Dancers who valued their careers were urged to drop out, and gradually he lost his cast. Misha, who as Hamlet was one of the most important players in the intrigue, continued to rehearse with Sergeyev. But he really didn't like the ballet, and after the first two performances he went with the tide and dropped out of the production. At a company meeting he fell into line, claiming publicly that he couldn't possibly continue to perform in the ridiculous choreography that Sergeyev had devised for him. Shortly afterward Sergeyev was dismissed and was replaced by a triumvirate directorship that included Kolpakova and her husband.

Things were looking good for Misha. He had been given a principal role in a new work by two young Bolshoi choreographers. The ballet, *Creation of the World*, was a light, lyrical play on the Genesis story, a pop version in which God creates the world out of boredom. Irina Kolpakova was cast as Eve, Valery Panov as the devil, Yuri Soloviev as God, and Baryshnikov as Adam. Misha loved the ballet. The role became one of his favorites, and it was a landmark in his career—it was, as he pointed out, his first serious work on a new production, "live with the choreographers." It was not an easy role, which made it all the more interesting for Misha. *Creation* made its debut in March 1971. The ballet opened with Adam as a baby, gazing innocently out over the audience, finding his feet and putting them into his mouth, making mud pies. Gradually he grew from within himself until, fully coordinated, he began to dance the awakening of adolescent experiences and finally the tragedy of adult life. It was a tragicomic role that suited Baryshnikov perfectly. He expressed a whole range of human emotions with intense sensitivity, and the public heart went out to him. Even Kolpakova seemed to warm to her partner. He wasn't a kid any more, he was a mature dancer.

Creation made a star dancer of Misha. *Fiesta*, a made-for-television movie with Baryshnikov in his first acting role, secured his place as a popular personality. The film, directed by one of Leningrad's most serious actors and based on Hemingway's *The Sun Also Rises*, cast Misha as the handsome young matador Pedro Romero. The movie was locked away after Baryshnikov's defection (although one party official did have it delivered to her home for a secret, private viewing), but those who saw it still remember Misha in the final scene, standing proudly in full matador's regalia, ready to meet his lonely fate.

Baryshnikov had proved himself. The darling of the Leningrad public, he was a charismatic hero too valuable to lose. When plans were made for a Kirov tour of Japan, the authorities thought twice before sending Misha. They observed him, investigated him, searched for an excuse to keep him safe at home. They even pulled in Valery Panov for questioning, offering him a chance to tour if he would give them the information they wanted about Baryshnikov. Panov, who hadn't left the country for ten years, refused, and Misha was sent to Japan. "It's impossible not to fall in love with that country," he told a Soviet journalist. "Its extraordinary mysteriousness, even a mythological quality, is enrapturing."

At the age of twenty-four Baryshnikov was being courted by one of the world's leading ballet companies. Since this was Soviet-style stardom, the material benefits were minimal, while privilege and recognition were everything. After the Japan tour Misha was given the role he most wanted. He wanted it because he knew they thought he couldn't do it. It was one of the greatest tests of a classical male dancer-actor—and it was the role that would follow him throughout his career, from Russia to the West.

In January 1972 Misha made his debut as Count Albrecht in *Giselle*. He was nervous. The history of the Kirov glittered with spectacular Albrechts, and everyone was waiting skeptically for Baryshnikov's attempt. His dancing was perfect, but how could this nice little guy play the unfeeling, aristocratic cad who disguises himself as a peasant in order to seduce the peasant girl Giselle?

Misha could scarcely believe in the traditional Albrecht. He doubted the character's stony heart and his repentance and transformation in the second act, after Giselle has died from the madness of a broken heart. In any case, he knew he couldn't play it that way. Misha could not imagine himself as a seducer; he was a young man just learning about love. And so a new Albrecht was born in Baryshnikov's self-image, one unlike any other. Misha's Albrecht did not see himself as a count any more than Misha saw himself as a ballet idol. He was just a romantic boy in love for the first time. Albrecht was human, sincere, impetuous, young enough to be stunned by his newly felt emotions, and stunned enough to forget that he was already engaged to be married to the duke's daughter, the lovely Bathilde. "It was total involvement, very raw," Misha remembers. The guilt of the traditional Albrecht was entirely missing; no moral message was involved.

Baryshnikov's brave new interpretation won the hearts of his audience. He was totally convincing, both in the innocence of his love and in the anguish of his realization that he has lost everything. Critics raved about Baryshnikov's performance; one called it "a sublime drama of the heart."

"To project passion was the easiest thing for me to do at that age," Baryshnikov said later in his career when his Albrecht was transformed by life's experiences. "It was the time of my first emotional involvement with women." At the age of twenty-four his "high school" romance with Tatyana Koltsova was developing into something more serious, and when the Kirov gave him a studio apartment to himself, Tanya moved in with him. By now she was dancing with the Kirov corps de ballet.

The apartment was in a beautiful section of central Leningrad, on the corner of the Griboyedov Canal and Dzerzhinsky Ulitsa, within walking distance of the theater and the Vaganova school. The apartment itself was small, dark, and uncomfortable, but after years of dormitories and communal apartments it was a home and privacy at last. A good friend gave Misha and Tanya a one-month-old poodle puppy named Foma, and a little later they were joined by Anfisa, a black cat.

Life should have been rosy. Misha was a star dancer living in the middle of Russia's most glorious cultural center. But comfortable jobs soon grow uncomfortable for ambitious people, and Misha was ambitious. He wanted to work, he wanted to experiment, he wanted to try everything. Without the challenge of the unfamiliar, how could he expand his art?

EIGHT

King of Infinite Space

THE MORE MISHA succeeded, the more he recognized that there was only so far he could go at the Kirov. He had danced Albrecht, and he would continue to dance Albrecht and Basil and the *Sleeping Beauty*'s prince month after month. There were no new challenges, nothing to excite him in the foreseeable future. There were no choreographers experimenting with new forms or ideas and little chance of anyone creating a new ballet for him. All he could see stretched before him were the same roles he had been dancing for months, and the same Kirov routine of meetings and backbiting and idleness.

Enforced idleness was traditional at the Kirov. Like all of the other dancers, past and present, Misha performed only three or four times a month. This wasn't policy—although it did result in dancers maturing more slowly and gently, with less burnout—it was simply that there were too many dancers for too few ballets. In Misha's day the Kirov repertoire was limited to twenty-six ballets. The situation was aggravated by the fact that the ballet company shared the theater with the opera, so performance time was limited. The Kirov was also suffering from a ballerina crisis, a shortage of female virtuoso talent spread thin among the several virtuoso male dancers. Misha still hadn't found the right partner. His height and youth made it almost impossible. How could he dance a love duet with a ballerina who was twenty years older or inches taller than he? A ballerina dancing on pointe adds six inches to her height. Tanya Koltsova, for instance, was taller than Misha when she stood on pointe.

Time was slipping by. Misha had begun to sense the possibilities that lay beyond the small world of the Kirov; and he was beginning to sense just how small that world was, and how unchangable. Slowly, excitement changed to boredom. He hated waiting. He hated the meetings and the secrecy and the compromising. It was a difficult time. Misha was a restless star, longing to break out. Tanya, in contrast, did her work in the corps when she had to; she didn't push herself. Misha would get tense and moody around her. He started drinking, and she didn't like him getting drunk. Sometimes when things didn't work out between them they would split up for a while, only to be drawn back together again. But Misha couldn't concentrate on Tanya. He was too filled with frustrated ambition. A year went by in this way. As Misha already knew, one year in a dancer's life is a long time, because a dancer's life is short.

In February 1972 George Balanchine brought the New York City Ballet to perform at his old home, the Kirov. Balanchine was a Vaganova Institute student when it was still called the Imperial Ballet School. He left the Maryinsky when he was a younger man than Misha was now and joined Diaghilev in Paris, taking the heritage to which Baryshnikov was heir and transforming it in the West into twentieth-century dance. Balanchine was the Picasso of ballet, and from the moment Misha first saw his work performed in Leningrad he sensed that this was the great future from which the frozen Russian ballet was hiding.

Misha loved Balanchine's tall, leggy ballerinas, and he couldn't take his eyes off one very young dancer in the company. Her name was Gelsey Kirkland. She was tiny and brilliant, with a childlike face, and when Misha saw her dance he knew that here at last was his ideal partner. Kirkland had heard of Baryshnikov, and although she didn't see him perform in Leningrad, she did see him at work in a Kirov class. She was stunned. This strange young man Baryshnikov was the best male dancer on the planet, she thought. She felt drawn to his genius but was too intimidated to approach him. She'd seen how the other men in the class cleared the floor for him and how people spoke his name in reverential whispers. He seemed inapproachable. How could she ever reach such heights of perfection? The perfection of the Russian dancers had both tantalized and frustrated Kirkland since she arrived in Moscow—so much so, in fact, that she'd begun to starve herself.

Misha attended all of the City Ballet performances. He met some of the dancers, who gave him news of Natalia Makarova— how well she was doing and how much money she was making, no mention of her sinking in the swamps of capitalism. One of the dancers, Peter Martins, told Misha he should leave Russia and go work with Balanchine in the New York City Ballet. Martins had done it—he'd left Denmark for Balanchine, and he'd never regretted it. But Misha just laughed and waved the idea away.

Balanchine took his company back to New York; John Cranko and the devoted and innovative Stuttgart Ballet came, performed, and left. Misha was hungry for the future, but it was slipping through his fingers. In the summer Tanya went to visit her mother, while Misha went with friends to relax at a rented dacha. It was a relief to be away from the hothouse atmosphere of the Kirov. It felt good to be surrounded by trees and grass, children, dogs, and warm friends. Misha let himself slip out of shape, he played, he fished. Then he left for a Spanish tour. He was on the list, even though he had avoided the company meetings and refused to condemn Panov as a traitor—Panov and his wife had just applied for permission to emigrate to Israel. Misha was happy to be going on tour. He and Koltsova met with some friends on the eve of his departure, and Misha got exuberantly drunk. But when he returned to Leningrad it was the same as before—no new works were planned and the dancers were dispirited. Even the Ministry of Culture was beginning to worry.

The feeling that the theater was a trap grew within Misha. It was a feeling that haunted other dancers, too. Some left to join provincial theaters or the Maly Theatre of Opera and Ballet in Leningrad, where the dancing was far from perfect but the work was more interesting. Misha's friend, the dancer Alexander (Sacha) Minz, managed to obtain permission to emigrate to the West; Misha took him to the airport and saw him off. Other equally talented dancers stayed and grew bitter. Misha could see it in the way they treated one another. Still, where could he go from the Kirov? For him, anywhere else in Russia would be a joke. He was twenty-four years old and had reached a dead end.

At the end of 1972 Misha submitted his resignation from the Kirov. He had no idea what he was going to do, he just knew he would no longer allow a bureaucracy to run his life. He intended to conduct his career in the way he thought best. Baryshnikov's impulsive decision to resign was sparked by an incident that centered on a televised production of *Giselle* in which, after months of boredom, he had been invited to dance. He had chosen as his partner the Bolshoi ballerina, Natalia Bessmertnova, wife of the Bolshoi's artistic director, Yuri Grigorovich. Bessmertnova was his perfect Giselle; with Makarova gone, no one could match her, not even at the Kirov. She was the best Giselle in the country. Misha was famous now, and he thought he should be able to choose his own partner. Taken aback by this open defiance of the established order, Rachinsky banned the couple from rehearsing. There were perfectly suitable ballerinas at the Kirov, he said. As it turned out, Misha's resignation was rejected within a day, and *Giselle* was televised with Baryshnikov and Bessmertnova. But Baryshnikov's first real stab at independence worried the authorities and alienated him even more from his cautious Kirov colleagues.

Misha's depression grew worse. Retreating behind a mask of indifference, his relationship with Koltsova deteriorated. Misha couldn't concentrate on domestic life. Now there were more bad times than good times. During the good times the couple talked about getting married, but as soon as they actually decided to do so, they split up for good. It was March 1973. Tanya moved out, taking Anfisa the cat with her. Misha moved with his faithful Foma—by now huge and shaggy—into a more spacious apartment that the theater had found for him. They were trying desperately to keep him happy; they even gave him a maid. Misha installed himself with his color television, his books, his music, and a few pieces of antique furniture inherited from Pushkin.

It was a beautiful apartment, part of what once had been a nobleman's residence. Misha had a bedroom, a tiny library, a kitchen, and a dining room all to himself. Outside there were trees and bushes, and the Moika Canal flowed by serenely; the little house of the poet Pushkin was across the street, the same house that Czar Nicholas I had ridden past day after day; and the Winter Palace was nearby. This was Leningrad's most desirable neighborhood. Baryshnikov had just turned twenty-five. His friends still lived in run-down or communal apartments.

Misha moved early in the spring. At the same time, yet another new artistic director was appointed to the Kirov, and Misha was given permission to prepare his own "creative evening"—a kind of safety valve for ambitious dancers. It looked hopeful. Misha was to have full control of his evening. He intended to collaborate with three of the country's most innovative choreographers; at last he would show the Kirov what could be done.

Misha's excitement was shortlived. He put six grueling months into his creation, working with choreographers, rehearsing his casts, directing set design, costume, and lighting. He was at work from morning till night, trying to coax the best out of a corps of bureaucratized ballet dancers who worked by the clock and didn't seem to care what they were dancing.

Even Koltsova was a problem. Misha had chosen her as his partner in one of the ballets he was preparing. He had never thought that she might feel uncomfortable working with her former lover; to Misha, work was one thing and pleasure was another. He thought he could turn Koltsova, who was still in the corps, into a ballerina. Not knowing how to deal with the situation, Koltsova sabotaged rehearsals by not showing up. Irina Kolpakova, who shared the role with her in the alternate cast, didn't attend a single rehearsal and finally dropped out. There were other fights with the administration over choices of ballerinas, costumes, and anything that varied from the norm.

By the end of the winter Misha was exhausted and hopelessly gloomy. He felt doomed to fail. He couldn't face himself or his friends. He was completely wrapped up in self-torment, accompanied by a self-proclaimed poet nicknamed "Suslik," who became Misha's shadow. The two went out drinking whenever Misha had a free night—to make Misha feel better, Suslik said when friends asked why he encouraged Misha's drinking. The friends that Misha had made over the past few years gave up on him. Ill-tempered and defensive, he was difficult to be with. He no longer called his friends, not wanting their company or advice as he always had in the past whenever he felt downcast. And they no longer called him because he was always with Suslik. They couldn't understand what bound those two together; they were worlds apart. Only after Misha's defection did it occur to Misha's friends that the shadowy Suslik might be a *stukach*, a KGB informant.

Baryshnikov's creative evening, in February 1974, was a sad affair. The public reception was good because Misha was dancing; tickets were sold out far in advance. But after the preview, at a meeting of the company establishment and its "official" critics, Misha was severely criticized. The choreography was too new, too modern; the casting was wrong; the ideas didn't work. Misha was sorely disappointed. He had tried so hard, and he was so tired, so fed up. Finally, at a thank-you reception that Misha held for the company, he broke down and cried in the middle of his speech. He simply could not pretend any more that he was happy. It didn't matter how many fans he had, how many times his name was whispered in adulation as he passed, how many pretty foreign ballet lovers besieged him after his performances. He was twenty-six years old, and the idea of dancing out his life at the Kirov made him miserable. He wanted to investigate new ways of moving; he wanted to dance to music by Webern. But they wouldn't let him.

The Kirov was frozen in the past, and Misha was looking to the future. In the weeks that followed, he tried to find a way out. With a new determination he pulled himself together, evaded Suslik, and saw his friends again. He thought about getting back together with Tanya. He bought a light-green Volga— sort of a cross between a Rambler and a Plymouth. There were possibilities in the air. Leonid Yacobson was planning a new ballet for Misha based on the commedia dell'arte. But then, so many of Yacobson's proposals already had been rejected—ballets based on the life of Mary Magdalen and on Picasso's paintings, among others. Then again, the French choreographer Roland Petit wanted Misha to go to Paris for a few months to work on a new ballet, and if they wouldn't allow him to do so, Petit said he would come to Leningrad and work with Misha on the Kirov stage. Petit's requests were turned down by the Ministry of Culture. Misha considered joining the Bolshoi Ballet and discussed it with his friends and with Grigorovich, the artistic director, who was in the process of negotiating a television production of his *Nutcracker* with Misha and Bessmertnova. Grigorovich had been the creative force behind the Kirov until he was pushed out with the promotion of Sergeyev. Misha respected him. When Grigorovich visited New York in 1987 he claimed that Baryshnikov had defected with a Bolshoi contract in his pocket. Baryshnikov neither affirmed nor denied that claim.

But in the spring of 1974 Misha had no plans to defect. He was too busy looking for a way to dance in Russia. After all, he wasn't a Solzhenitsyn, a Sakharov, or even a Panov, suffering under Soviet rule. He was just a frustrated ballet idol looking for a little bit of artistic freedom.

Yet the more he succeeded, the more he was expected to conform and involve himself in public affairs, and the more uncomfortable he felt. As a beloved young star it was Baryshnikov's responsibility to set an example for his Soviet peers. At the end of 1973 he was given a title: Honored Artist of the Soviet Socialist Republic. This was both a privilege and a trap—the title proclaimed him a respected and exemplary citizen. Misha didn't feel like an exemplary citizen. He hated politics, had never believed in his father's Stalinism, and, as he put it later, thought "the system sucked." He hated to compromise his attitudes and make a lie of his life, but sometimes he did just that because his career depended on it. When he was told to attend a Kosmosol congress in Moscow (a meeting of the Young Communist League) he went, but sat gloomily in his suit and tie while the other young people made uplifting speeches. It made him angry. He felt it was stupid for him to be there when he could have been rehearsing *Giselle* with Kolpakova instead.

On April 30 Baryshnikov performed *Giselle* with Natalia
Bessmertnova on the Kirov stage. He had been dancing this role
repeatedly for three years now, and although his Albrecht was
still spectacularly eloquent, remarkably young, and very much in
love, the heartbreaking innocence that marked his debut had
been replaced by a growing anguish at the loss of *Giselle*. Tonight
Misha's bitterly hopeless Albrecht left the audience stunned. The
image of torment penetrated his every movement until the curtain closed, leaving him on his knees in the center of the stage,
surrounded by pure void. Friends who saw the performance remember it as a powerful foreboding. This was Baryshnikov's last
performance on the Kirov stage.

The Bolshoi was planning a tour of Canada in June 1974.
Since the company was scheduled to perform in London at the
same time, Canada was left with the dregs, a second-string
troupe of dancers due for retirement. Irina Kolpakova was picked
to add a little zest to the tour, and they wanted to send Baryshnikov, too. Both dancers were free, since the Kirov tour to the
United States scheduled for July had been cancelled because of
the energy crisis and, although this was not officially stated,
over the Soviet government's treatment of Valery Panov. But the
authorities had serious reservations about Baryshnikov. They
simply did not trust him any more.

Irina Kolpakova, who was entirely above suspicion, made the
final difference by promising to take responsibility for Misha's
safe return. Then the gossip started. Would Baryshnikov come
back, or would he follow Makarova and Nureyev to the West?
Some of Misha's best friends hoped that he would not return.
Already they had watched the happy, excited boy they once
knew grow gaunt and tired. They saw no future for him in Russia. But for all their subtle suggestions, Misha seemed sincere
when he said he had no intention of staying in the West. The
thought of never coming back was almost impossible for him to
imagine. Besides, Misha had seen enough of Western ballet to

know that it was very different than what he knew, and he wondered if he could adapt. He didn't want to become a second-rate dancer. He'd been the best for too long.

Even so, as the time to leave approached, Misha became strangely silent. At one point, out of the blue, he asked his friend Gennady Shmakov, "Do you think that if I worked, let's say, in New York, I'd be successful?"

On the eve of his departure Misha called Tatyana Koltsova. They talked for a long time. Tanya wanted to hang up because she was uncomfortable sitting for so long on the floor of the corridor where the phone was, but Misha wouldn't let her go. The next day Misha called Suslik from the airport. Then he flew to Moscow to join the Bolshoi dancers for their flight to Toronto. It was going to be a joke of a tour. As John Fraser, a Canadian journalist, put it, the troupe was made up of a "rag-tag collection of provincial second-raters and overage establishment loyalists." The tour leaders, Alexander Lapauri and his wife Raissa Struchkova, were little more than burly watchdogs.

Nevertheless, critics and fans alike traveled from New York to see the Bolshoi perform at Toronto's O'Keefe Center. They came to see Baryshnikov. They were intrigued—was he really a genius? If so, what kind of a genius was he? The dance critics Clive and Patricia Barnes went to see him. They had a message for him, but they couldn't get close. Baryshnikov was being protected. In Toronto, John Fraser tried to arrange an interview with Misha but Lapauri refused him permission.

Gelsey Kirkland, Peter Martins, and a fellow dancer named Victor Barbee traveled to Toronto to see Baryshnikov. Because the three were staying in the same hotel as Misha, Martins took the opportunity to invite him to dinner. Misha's English was minimal, but with a pat on the backside and a few words he managed to tell Kirkland that she would make a perfect partner for him. She was embarrassed. She thought it was a joke, or a pass, or both. Martins tried to tell Misha he should stay and dance in the West, with Balanchine's New York City Ballet. As soon as the subject came up, Misha turned away, flustered. He didn't want to talk about it. Martins assumed that Misha was being watched. He was excited, convinced that Misha would defect, leaving him free to join the City Ballet. And what an inspiration it would be to have Baryshnikov in the company!

Meanwhile, Clive Barnes had contacted John Fraser, asking him to convey an urgent message to Baryshnikov. The message was simple: a New York City phone number. Three of Misha's friends—Sacha Minz, Christina Berlin, and a Russian ballet photographer living in New York, Dina Makarova—were anxious for him to contact them. Fraser planned to catch Baryshnikov at a reception after the performance on the twenty-fourth. He figured out a way of passing the message to Misha by taping it to the inside of a ring. He was very nervous.

Misha was there, looking tired and bored, seated at a huge table with the Lapauris, the director of the National Ballet of Canada, and translators, who Fraser suspected were really KGB agents. When Fraser finally caught Misha alone and gave him the message, Misha's face lit up. He was surprised and pleased, which in itself seemed to make Lapauri suspicious enough to ask Misha how much the Canadians had offered him to join their company. Obviously, Baryshnikov's dissatisfaction was a source of bitter amusement by now among the Russian dancers. "Half a million," Misha replied cynically. "But I'm holding out for more." Less than a week later, Fraser heard the news of Baryshnikov's defection.

He didn't decide until the last moment. Minz and Dina Makarova had come from New York and had talked. Alone, Baryshnikov probably would not have been able to do more than ponder the possibility of not going home. But Minz was a good friend who made the notion seem less lonely, and Makarova knew the ballet world inside out. It's hard to defect without someone on your side. Nureyev did it on his first tour by jumping over the barrier at the Paris airport, but Nureyev had always been in trouble with the authorities, from the time he became a Vaganova student to the time he left the Kirov. Misha wasn't Nureyev. Misha was careful and objective. He needed information, advice, and assurances.

A young general lawyer named Jim Peterson agreed to work with Baryshnikov. He had never dealt with a defection before. Peterson met with Misha and they talked; at first he just wanted to be sure that Misha knew what he was doing. He didn't want him to change his mind at the last moment. Then he explained the process. It was up to Misha to make the final decision. Until then, any plans were tentative.

Suddenly the possibility was so close. Before it had always been an abstract idea, but now the reality of the dilemma was almost overwhelming. It wasn't just a question of risk—although he knew they were keeping an eye on him on this tour. He knew the price of being caught, too. A traitor to the homeland, he would be sentenced to fifteen years in jail for treason, and the rest of his life would be wasted in some frozen region of the country. He would never dance again. And there was the risk to his friends. Would they be harassed, dragged into the Big House—the Leningrad KGB headquarters—for questioning, have their phones tapped and their privileges curtailed? What about his father? But he had scarcely seen his father in years. They couldn't blame him for his errant son. Irina Kolpakova had guaranteed his return. Would she be blamed?

On June 29 the plan had already been in place for two days, and for two days Misha had been wavering on the verge of a decision. The last performance in Toronto was tonight, and after that it would be too late. Everyone was waiting for him to decide, but Misha had to be sure. It wasn't the risk that kept him pacing. Misha was a kid running away from a very safe home. For the first time in his life he was making a crucial choice about his life, a choice with which he alone would have to live. Misha was about to leave Foma, his friends, his apartment, his books, his records, his pictures, the language, the faces, and the white nights and frosts and spires of Leningrad that he'd loved almost before he first saw them eleven years ago, and he would never be able to go back, even if he wanted to go back. What lay ahead? It was a huge, unknown world that he didn't really understand. It was an exciting world, full of possibilities. But could it ever be home?

Misha couldn't be sure, but he had to take the risk of being wrong. He wished he didn't have to. He wished he could go back and live and dance and save everybody all of the trouble he was going to cause, but they wouldn't let him develop and he knew he would suffocate. It was a tragedy. Already he could feel a rootlessness sapping his spirit. Already he was homesick. Yet it was exciting, too; he had decided, and now there was a whole new world waiting for him.

Misha made a call to Christina Berlin in London, where she was working with *Cosmopolitan* magazine, and asked her to come. She rushed to the airport—she would rush anywhere for Misha. The banks were closed and she didn't have cash for a ticket to Toronto, so she stopped passersby and begged them to cash personal checks. When she had enough money, she bought a ticket and took the first flight out. Natalia Makarova was in London, too, dancing with the Royal Ballet. Misha called her for advice. Surely, Natasha could help him find work, introduce him, support him in his choice—she had done it first. But Makarova wasn't there. At that moment she was dancing *Giselle* at Covent Garden. She would be back later, after Misha had defected.

But first he had to dance. It would be a hundred times harder than dancing through an injury. He was trembling, his stomach was turning, he was drained and wired. The way Misha looked now, there was a risk he might give himself away before he even reached the stage. He knew that the only thing he could do was to dance until it was time to perform. The discipline would do him good. Tomorrow the company would leave for Vancouver. Tonight he would dance, take his last bow with the Russian ballet, and quickly make his escape. He had decided, and he was terrified. Trembling, Misha left for the theater.

NINE

Dreams and Nightmares

 FOR MIKHAIL BARYSHNIKOV, on the morning of Sunday, June 30, the world was strangely quiet. All around him was the stillness of trees and grass. The terrible suspense of last night's performance, the wild chase through the night streets of Toronto, the near miss with the passing car, the final escape from the city—it was all over. Except for the feeling that still gripped him. He had made a huge leap, and he hadn't landed yet.

Misha knew that the calm was illusory. Back in Toronto, not so many miles away from this isolated farmhouse where he had driven last night with Berlin, Dina Makarova, Minz, and Peterson, today must be pure frenzy. This morning, while he waited in hiding, the rest of the troupe would be packing up and flying to Vancouver. Who would be blamed for the fiasco of his defection? They already would have talked to Moscow. Peterson had notified the Canadian authorities, but nothing was finalized yet. Soon the Canadians would be contacting the embassy in Ottowa. In Leningrad the KGB would be turning his life upside

down in a mad search for clues. The Canadian police were looking for him, and probably the KGB was, too. Even though everything around him looked so quiet, perhaps at this very
moment they were nearing the farmhouse.

Inside the farmhouse, everyone was nervous. Tina was elated
to be with Misha again, though he was not easy to be with. She
had never seen him like this. One moment he was elated, the
next he was full of torment. At times he was distant. She began
to feel unsure of herself.

Peterson had assumed responsibility for keeping Misha safely
hidden away while he dealt with the official papers that would
guarantee the dancer's security in Canada. The safe house where
they were staying belonged to his friends. Now the wheels were
in motion; they had prepared a press statement on behalf of
Misha, briefly explaining his motives for defecting. Tomorrow
the story would break in the papers and then reporters would be
out looking for Baryshnikov. Peterson was worried. He knew
they couldn't leave the farmhouse and had to use the telephone
with care. This was a small, rural community with a small, rural
exchange. Anyone could be watching or listening in.

While Peterson took care of the papers, Misha tried to plan.
He knew that in order to stay sane, he had to work. Right now
he was in limbo. He was a citizen of no nation, a member of no
company, and he had no partner. He was simply in hiding. But
the wheels were in motion.

Today Natalia Makarova was on her way to New York City
for the debut of her staging of *La Bayadere* for American Ballet
Theatre. He'd finally managed to contact her in London at midnight, almost as soon as they had arrived at the farmhouse. It
was five o'clock in the morning London time when Natalia's
phone rang. She was still exhausted after her final evening performance of *Giselle* with the Royal Ballet, and she was nervous
about her first attempt at staging a ballet. Misha sounded upset.
He was stammering.

Overjoyed to hear Misha's voice, Natalia had happily agreed

to talk to Lucia Chase, the director of American Ballet Theatre, the moment she arrived in New York. "I realized," recalls Makarova, "that for a dancer like Misha, ABT was the only place in America where he could immediately display his phenomenal technique and artistry." Natalia was confident that she could arrange for Misha to partner her in some performances during the coming ABT season. But when could he start? She had mentioned the premiere of *La Bayadere*, yet that was in only two days time; it would take about three weeks for his U.S. immigration papers to be processed. The next opportunity was July 27, partnering Natalia in a performance of *Giselle*, if her scheduled partner, Ivan Nagy, would permit it. So Misha had four weeks to kill.

It was impossible for Misha to relax. Amid his anxieties about being discovered, his excitement, and his sense of loss, he couldn't forget Gelsey Kirkland. Much as he wanted to dance with Natalia, he knew that Kirkland would be a perfect partner for him. Of course, she would have to leave Balanchine and the New York City Ballet. Misha wanted to find out; he couldn't wait. On Sunday afternoon, he asked Dina to call Kirkland.

Gelsey Kirkland was working out at the side of the stage in the theater at Lincoln Center when she received Misha's call. Being Sunday, the building was practically deserted. She was working overtime—trying to heal the wound of a messed-up love affair by dancing. On Sunday, June 30, Kirkland was trying to erase Peter Martins from her mind. Since their trip to Toronto to see Baryshnikov perform two weeks ago, things had fallen apart between them. According to Kirkland in *Dancing on My Grave*, it was a classic love triangle, with Martins bouncing from Kirkland to his former girlfriend, ballerina Heather Watts. It was Kirkland who had broken off the relationship—and with it their plans for escaping together from the "dead end" of the New York City Ballet.

The City Ballet had been her second family for as long as she could remember—she had started in the company's school at the age of eight and became Balanchine's "baby ballerina." It was a safe and familiar life, but she despised it. Martins had provided her with the courage to break away. "The problem was," writes Kirkland, "I didn't know how to think of my future in ballet without him." For her, a dance partner and a lover had always been one and the same.

When Kirkland was called from the stage to take a long distance phone call she had no expectations. She wasn't at all surprised to hear Dina Makarova's voice on the other end of the line—they had known each other for years. But today Dina's voice had "a ring of excitement," and she came to the point quickly. Baryshnikov, Dina explained, had defected, and she had been called in to interpret for him. The press knew nothing yet, and Kirkland was to tell noboby. Misha wanted to know if Gelsey would dance with him. That was it; Misha wanted to know. Practically tongue-tied, she listened as Misha took the phone and said a few hesitant words in English. It was beyond her wildest dreams. She could scarcely contain herself.

By the next day, Monday, July 1, the news was out. A front-page *New York Times* story, peppered with dramatic eye-witness accounts, disclosed that Mikhail Baryshnikov, one of the world's leading male ballet dancers, who had fled the Bolshoi "apparently to continue dancing in the West," had defected. Baryshnikov, the report said, was accompanied by Christina Berlin, "a close friend." There was a "no comment" from the embassy. The story in the *New York Post* went further. That article, relegated to page nine, was headlined, "Soviet Dancer Leaps West," and stated that "police were tight-lipped about the incident. But informed sources here said police were on the watch for Baryshnikov throughout Canada and especially in the Toronto area."

Of course, it was wonderful for Canada to have a great Russian dancer land on her doorstep, but it was also politically embarrassing. Baryshnikov's defection could only aggravate East-West cultural relations, which were already strained by the anti-Soviet demonstrations that had marred the June performances of

Russian dance troupes in London and New York. Misha had been aware of the politically charged atmosphere surrounding Soviet ballet in the West even before his defection. Anti-Soviet chants from the audience had almost disrupted one of his performances in Canada, and he'd heard that demonstrators had released mice into the audience at a Bolshoi performance in London just a few days earlier; in New York, stink bombs had been set off during a Moiseyev dance troupe appearance. Baryshnikov's defection at this time put the Canadians in a difficult situation—whether it was described as a politically or artistically motivated act hardly mattered. After all, in the eyes of the Soviet Union he had just committed a criminal act. Misha knew that by now in Leningrad they would be calling him a traitor.

In fact, Misha's friends in Leningrad first heard of his disappearance at eight o'clock on Monday morning over the "naughty voice"—the Voice of America. At first nobody could think what might have happened to Misha. By eleven o'clock on the morning of the first, the KGB had contacted his closest friends, including Nina Alovert, with invitations to appear at the Big House that afternoon. The KGB were convinced that Baryshnikov had been persuaded by his friends to defect. In fact, it suspected a conspiracy, and it wanted to know who was responsible. The KGB also wanted Misha's friends to write letters urging him to come back home. The investigation continued unsuccessfully for a few days, phones were tapped, and then the affair lapsed into silence.

On Tuesday Misha received a special permit allowing him to remain in Canada for six months. This was renewable for another six-month period. Officially, his future was taking shape. He could come out of hiding, pick up his permit, and carry on with his life. But he was in no hurry to come out into the open. Peterson thought it would be safer if he were to stay in the farmhouse for a few more days until his situation was absolutely secure. Misha was still afraid. The Soviet embassy in Ottawa had requested assistance from the Canadian Department of External Affairs in having a representative meet and talk to Baryshnikov. They obviously had not given up on him yet. Misha refused. They teased him. They let him know that he had been given special status in Russia and that he would not be prosecuted if he returned. So he could change his mind and go back now if he wanted. They were giving him a choice, confusing his already troubled mind. But again Misha refused. For the first time in his life he could say no to the Russian government. Maybe he would turn out to be wrong, but at least he was making his own decisions. When a reporter asked a spokesman for the Bolshoi troupe, now in Vancouver, how they felt about losing their leading dancer, he replied sourly, "we have no stars."

In Leningrad, the KGB spread rumors that Baryshnikov had merely accepted an invitation to work in the West for a couple of years. They even kept his apartment in order to support the story. This way, they thought, perhaps everyone would quietly forget about Baryshnikov. All over the Soviet Union, even in Riga, posters of the nation's favorite ballet idol were removed from the streets. Soon Baryshnikov's name would be removed from books and his image on film and tape locked away. Irina Kolpakova was quickly forgiven, but Lapauri was banned from further tours.

In the States, barely a day went by without a newspaper report about the progress and plans of Mikhail Baryshnikov. In the absence of a statement from Misha, gossip and speculation were spreading fast. By Tuesday, rumors of Misha's desire to dance with Gelsey Kirkland appeared in Clive Barnes's *New York Times* dance column. It was only two days since Dina Makarova had called Kirkland on Misha's behalf, stressing secrecy. The news came at the end of a review of the New York City Ballet's season finale, in which Barnes praised Kirkland's "delicate and absorbing" performance. "The two of them would make a potent combination," he predicted.

On Thursday a Soviet aide in Ottawa released a statement

through the press, claiming that Baryshnikov had been abducted by an American woman and had been tempted to perform for "private enterprise." "Baryshnikov was a poor boy at home," the official said, "and I'm sure they promised him that he would earn more money." He claimed that the dancer already had plans to dance with the Canadian ballet in New York. In response, David Haber, artistic director of the National Ballet of Canada, was quoted as saying that he would be "delighted, and not too surprised," if Baryshnikov decided to join his company. He said that during the week preceding his defection, Misha had visited several company rehearsals and had seemed "unusually impressed."

Misha was unaccustomed to the ways of the Western press. In Russia he had given only one newspaper interview, despite the fact that he was an idol of the Soviet ballet world. His performances had been reviewed, but his life was his own. Nevertheless, he could see that silence would do him no good. The only way to put the record straight was through the press. So when John Fraser called the farmhouse and asked for an exclusive interview, Misha agreed.

Fraser had learned about the defection in Newfoundland, where he had gone for a short vacation on the very night of Baryshnikov's flight, only five days after furtively passing Misha the crucial message at the O'Keefe Center reception. He knew the farmhouse where Misha was being hidden—Jim Peterson's friends, the owners, were friends of Fraser's, too. He arrived, straight from Newfoundland, to find the atmosphere in the safe house charged with tension. "The three of them," he recalled twelve years later in a memoir, "were showing signs of being cooped up together for too long." The atmosphere, both inside and outside, was heavy. Thunderstorms were brewing, and the air was hot and steamy.

Apparently, Misha had been irritable. He had dark circles under his eyes. Night after night he had been waking up in a shivering sweat, plagued by nightmares. As he would put it several years later, Misha had turned "from the very firm and nice road" of familiar Leningrad "to the swamp" of unknown territories. For everyone in the house, each moment was like walking on eggs. Misha was liable to crack.

Christina Berlin struck Fraser as "beautiful and emotionally fragile." She was also, by most accounts, desperately in love with Misha. It was an unfortunate combination. What she must have hoped might be a few weeks of bliss in a romantic hideaway was quickly turning into an icy situation. Misha had a way, at times, of creating an immense distance between them. Berlin had been dealing with the situation by cooking and caring for Misha. She was also teaching him English.

Although Berlin would back up Baryshnikov's official press statement that they were "just good friends," to John Fraser she announced that she and Misha were already, in effect, married. "The more she insisted," recalls Fraser, "the less sure Misha became." In the days ahead the situation only grew worse.

Misha knew what he wanted. He wanted the freedom to dance with ballet companies all over the world, he wanted to work with choreographers who would challenge his abilities, he wanted to partner ballerinas like Natalia Makarova and Gelsey Kirkland, and to try out different dance forms while still dancing the classics for which he had been so superbly trained. Most of all, he wanted to perform in ballets by George Balanchine and Jerome Robbins, although he knew that he lacked the training and that Balanchine had a strict no-star policy. Besides, he had no intention, he told Fraser, of permanently joining a ballet company—not the National Ballet of Canada or any other.

It was pointed out that Baryshnikov would make much more money by guesting with various companies than by becoming a permanent member of any one. But it wasn't the money that made him want this freedom, just as it wasn't money that had motivated his defection. He hadn't been poor at home, he insisted, and he hadn't been politically suppressed in any way. In fact, he had been treated very well. It was only that he wanted to work with foreign troupes, to fulfill his artistic ambitions, and they wouldn't let him. "He was spoiled rotten," recalls Fraser. After all, he was already a superstar and he was only twenty-six years old.

Fraser's interview was published in the *Toronto Globe and Mail* on Saturday, July 6, exactly one week after Misha's defection. On the same day, Clive Barnes, writing in *The New York Times*, upgraded his description of Baryshnikov from a "leading dancer" to "superstar." In the course of seven days the American press had elevated a great Soviet dancer to heavenly stature. Now they went out in search of the man himself. He was already a personality, offering the promise of a hot, romantic story. Not only was he a great ballet dancer, possibly the greatest in the world, he was also a mysterious Russian and a defector; he was hiding out with a beautiful woman; he was attractive, even sexy, in a boy-next-door kind of a way; and, best of all, he apparently was not gay. The story was so hot that reporters from a rival paper had already entered John Fraser's Toronto apartment—he was in the habit of leaving his key under the front doormat— and ransacked his papers, looking for exclusive information on the mysterious dancer.

Once the *Toronto Globe and Mail* story was printed, Misha began to venture out into the world. His nerves were still sorely strained; he soothed them by fishing and walking in the woods. He summoned up the courage to travel daily into Toronto for class; although he was still terrified by the thought of being snatched away by the KGB, he knew he had to keep his body in shape. Out of politeness to the Canadians he had agreed that his postdefection debut should be in Canada. It was decided after negotiations that Baryshnikov would dance the role of James in a Canadian television production of Auguste Bournonville's *La Sylphide*. The possibility of Misha partnering Makarova in the National Ballet's New York performance of Nureyev's new *Sleeping Beauty* was suggested but quickly forgotten. Naturally,

Nureyev wasn't prepared to give up his role as Prince Florimund for this new defector.

The prospect of performing in *La Sylphide* was just what Misha needed. He had never danced the role before, so he had plenty to learn, plenty to occupy his time in the days ahead. Dancing easily became his emotional outlet. Meanwhile, negotiations with American Ballet Theatre were coming to a close, thanks to the efforts of Natalia Makarova. Ivan Nagy, ever courteous, had agreed to let Misha take his place as Albrecht, partnering Makarova's Giselle on July 27. This was to be Makarova's only performance of *Giselle* this season. Baryshnikov would also dance with Makarova in her new staging of the "Kingdom of the Shades" scene from *La Bayadere* on August 5, and in the *Don Quixote* pas de deux on August 9. After that he would guest in ABT's season at the Kennedy Center in Washington, D.C., beginning in late October and in the company's January season in New York. Dancing with the ABT, with its huge, eclectic repertoire, was something Misha looked forward to.

With new roles to learn, rehearsals to attend, and daily classes, the next few months were pretty well sewn up. All that remained was for Gelsey Kirkland to negotiate some kind of arrangement with ABT for the coming season. And of course there was New York to look forward to—the very center of what, back home, was called the "evil empire."

In New York, Kirkland had decided that whether or not things worked out with Baryshnikov, she was going to leave the New York City Ballet. If Misha, whom she respected above all others, had found the courage to leave his home and everything he knew, then so could she. The company traveled for its summer season to Saratoga, upstate New York, and while there, Kirkland broke the news to Balanchine. She didn't mention anything about Baryshnikov.

From Saratoga, Gelsey called Misha in Canada. Through Dina Makarova they spoke excitedly about their plans. "Each call was a variation on the same theme: his desire to dance with me," wrote Kirkland in her autobiography. "I had somehow become a part of his plans. . . . He had seen me dance in Russia. . . . He believed in me." During one of their phone conversations, Misha told her that he had a picture of her with him. This was enough to send Gelsey's heart racing. Did Misha have more than a dance partnership in mind?

As the summer heated up, so did the stories in the press. Not only had a major personality just landed on the doorstep of America, but now he was causing huge upheavals in the world of dance. Gelsey Kirkland's plan to leave Balanchine for Baryshnikov and the rival ABT was major news. It was almost another defection. Balanchine responded with subtle denigration: "Every dancer secretly wants to be Giselle," he told *Newsweek* disparagingly on July 29, 1974. Riding high through the stormy heat of that extraordinarily hot summer, Kirkland waited with keen anticipation to take her turn with Misha.

TEN

Gelsey

HAVING SUCCESSFULLY PERFORMED *La Sylphide* for Canadian television, Misha arrived in New York City around the middle of July. Berlin had gone on ahead, ostensibly to arrange things for Misha. He had been granted an H1 visa on account on his special abilities; he was without citizenship and without a home, but here he was in the United States of America.

For a new arriver, Misha had an easy time in New York. He landed, as he put it, "squarely on two feet." Everyone wanted to help. He was invited to parties, to country houses, to openings, and to dinners. He was offered temporary homes in the city with his friend Sacha Minz and with Helen and Sheldon Atlas. Helen was then the editor of *Dance News*. But before long he met the multimillionaire Howard Gilman, chairman of the board of Gilman Paper Company and a renowned patron of the arts. One of the many rich and influential businessmen who were attracted to Baryshnikov's very different glamor, Gilman invited the dancer to share his luxury penthouse apartment on Fifty-seventh

Street—Misha had a suite to himself. "The atmosphere," says Kirkland in *Dancing on My Grave*, "was on the order of a hotel suite, all rather anonymous and impersonal." But it was comfortable, easy, and air-conditioned. Misha entered directly into the high life of New York City, with its attendant gossip columnists, hangers on, groupies, and would-be friends. Mikhail Baryshnikov was an international celebrity.

Before he had even set foot in the United States, Baryshnikov's name had traveled far wider than the usual ballet circles. As early as July 11 the news of his engagements at ABT with Natalia Makarova had been leaked to the press, along with a picture of Baryshnikov and Berlin together. On the steamy hot morning of July 12, before the box office opened at ten o'clock, a long line had already formed outside the New York State Theater. The line grew throughout the morning, snaking around the theater lobby, swelling into the street, and breaking police lines. Some people waited as long as two-and-a-half hours for tickets in the sweltering heat. Well before closing, the box office had sold all of its 2,779 seats for *Giselle*. For an American ballet company in 1974, this kind of response was the stuff of dreams. No one had ever seen anything like it. Even ABT, America's leading company along with the City Ballet, had been struggling for years to make ends meet. In the newspapers the next day, Misha's incredible box office success became the latest Baryshnikov news story. And he hadn't yet set foot on an American stage.

On the evening of July 27 ticketless fans gathered again before the performance of *Giselle* in the hope of last minute cancellations. Outside the theater scalpers were selling tickets for as much as fifty dollars apiece. Inside, every seat was filled. "The Hamptons," wrote critic John Rockwell, referring to the favorite summer retreat of New York's well-to-do, "for once on a late July weekend, must have been empty."

The excited anticipation on the part of his first American audience created a real challenge for Misha. He had arrived in

New York with only a few days to rehearse for the performance, and he knew that the entire dance world would be watching him, ready to judge. Besides, he had never partnered Makarova in *Giselle*—he'd had very little opportunity to dance with her at the Kirov—and he was unfamiliar with the State Theater stage. On the other hand, Makarova was probably the best Giselle of her day. She still knew all of the variations of the ballet as it was performed by the Kirov and she had no problem modifying her own interpretation to suit Misha. She was ready to give up the evening to him; she must have known that whether he wanted it or not, the spotlight would be his. Besides, she wanted their partnership to start on a good note. "He suits me so much," said Makarova. "It's like a marriage."

Makarova had high hopes for their partnership and for their friendship. "Our reunion was filled with emotion," she recalls in her autobiography. "We hadn't seen each other for four years." Since her sudden flight from the 1970 Kirov tour in London, Misha had grown. He wasn't a boy any more. As a partner he was stronger and more confident. As they rehearsed daily for *Giselle*, Makarova began to feel the electricity flow. "It's as if we charge each other with voltage," she said.

Meanwhile, Kirkland, still in Saratoga, remained cautiously optimistic. She was thinking about Misha as he prepared for *Giselle*; before the performance she sent him a telegram reading, "Misha, Merde a million times, much love Gelsey." In the world of ballet, *merde* means good luck.

On the night of July 27 security was tight at Lincoln Center. Members of the orchestra were escorted into the pit one by one as a special security measure. Misha was tense. He didn't like to be seen as a defector; he was just a dancer. He thought people would be expecting too much after all that had been written. And he couldn't understand what anyone was saying.

The performance began just after eight o'clock, and immediately there was magic in the air. "It was as if we were in a trance," recalls Makarova. "We seemed in some way possessed, taken over by the dancing as if it had a life outside ourselves." The critics agreed: "Their Giselle and Albrecht," wrote Arlene Croce in her review, "were as psychically fused as Cathy and Heathcliff." It was pure romance. And yet, said Croce, perhaps Makarova needed a partner who could devote himself to her more completely, someone like Ivan Nagy.

Not until ten o'clock, with Misha's first big solo of the evening in act two, did the audience finally witness Baryshnikov in his full, soaring splendor. The audience gasped. Suddenly the stage of the State Theater was, as Anna Kisselgoff put it in her glowing review, "simply too small for Mr. Baryshnikov." A violinist in the orchestra became so excited that he almost threw his instrument onstage.

As the performance ended, Misha's instant fans rose for thirty wild minutes of standing ovations. There were twenty-four curtain calls. Dozens of bouquets littered the stage floor, and the auditorium was filled with shouts of "Misha! Misha! Misha!" They were thrilled by him. Even as he stood, smiling nervously on the stage while they called for him, he endeared himself to his new fans. Dancing he was a god, he soared; the moment he landed he became mortal again, and as a mortal he seemed tantalizingly available.

The critics were equally as awed by Baryshnikov's performance. They found in him not only the most perfect classical technique but also great originality in the way he made that technique his own by inventing personal variations to the steps. He was just about as perfect as any dancer could be. Even while performing the most difficult of steps, technical feats that only half a dozen dancers in the world were capable of, he maintained that level of perfection. His body was a moving sculpture, always composed, even in mid air. Yet there was never any sign of the effort involved; he made it look so easy. It was exhilarating. "He blasted off with the hesitation and majesty of a spaceship. He turned—once, twice—and every thread on his costume was plainly visible as he soared high above the audience like an astronaut looking back at earth," said Hubert Saal in a *Newsweek* review on August 12, 1974. He was unbelievable.

Before the performance a few critics had questioned Baryshnikov's choice of *Giselle* as his American debut. After all, they pointed out, *Giselle* is a ballerina's ballet. Until the second act, the role of Albrecht doesn't have much scope for a dancer like Baryshnikov to display his virtuosity. Albrecht had always been a strictly partnering role, with the male dancer lifting the ballerina and showing her off.

Yet, the critics realized, Misha had managed to make the male role something more, simply through his own interpretation of Albrecht's character. They had never seen such an Albrecht. Misha had taken Giselle's anguish and made it his own. Only the week before, right across the street at the Uris Theater, Nureyev had performed the same role with the National Ballet of Canada. His Albrecht had been entirely different—sensual, sophisticated, and, finally, filled with guilt. Misha's love for Giselle was heartrendingly innocent. He was irresistibly lost without her. His grief attracted empathy. "He brought to his interpretation," said Hubert Saal in *Newsweek*, "a terrifying intensity that never relaxed." In fact, a couple of critics ventured, perhaps the expression of emotion was just a little bit—overdone.

Baryshnikov followed his American debut with three performances near the beginning of August, including a surprise appearance on August 6 that left ticketholders speechless with disbelief. Misha, now dubbed "the hottest thing on two legs," danced with Natalia Makarova in all three performances, and the ballet world began to see them as an established, long-term partnership. Perhaps, people thought, here was another Nureyev and Fonteyn. "They go so well together," wrote Clive Barnes, "she looks naughty and he looks surprised." It was Misha who gave her the naughty glint in her eyes.

But in the shadow of Makarova's delight, Kirkland was still waiting. She had returned to New York near the beginning of August and had begun on a feverish body-improvement campaign—working out, dieting, and practicing in the dance studio. Misha was a star and a genius, and she felt she had to make herself worthy of him. It hardly mattered to Kirkland that she had been singled out as an exceptional dancer in her own right—as a principal in the New York City Ballet at the age of nineteen, she had received her share of adulation from the press. It hardly mattered, because Kirkland had never been the ballerina—or the woman—she'd wanted to be. She'd already had silicone implanted into her breasts and lips, and after visiting Russia with Balanchine she'd tried almost neurotically to remodel herself in the image of a Russian ballerina. Natalia Makarova had been her model of perfection, her idol. As far as Gelsey was concerned, Natasha was the greatest ballerina in the world. She had been the source of both her inspiration and her frustration. Now she felt sure that in partnering Misha, she would be compared to Makarova. She felt like a waif.

By the time Baryshnikov and Kirkland met in New York near the beginning of August, both dancers had made their separate deals with ABT. Kirkland was to appear in at least half of Baryshnikov's performances, but no details had been worked out yet. In the following weeks their personal relationship developed faster than their partnership plans. Kirkland felt both thrilled and confused. She claims that in public Baryshnikov more or less ignored her, while in private he remained emotionally distant. She felt there was more than a language problem. "By dancing between amorous partners, withholding his commitment to anyone in particular," she states, "he constructed his own iron curtain, drawn as a precaution against the hazards of love and attachment."

Gelsey was ready to forgive Misha his apparent insensitivity toward the women close to him. She saw his cool behavior toward Makarova first and then Berlin—witnessed on her first two dates with Misha—as a kind of a complex game in which she was the winner. She also held a romantic image of Baryshnikov as a homeless, suffering artist, an image which made him and his weaknesses all the more alluring.

The press had already latched onto this image and had done its best to propagate it. Now that Baryshnikov was in New York, there was a spate of articles and interviews. The time was ripe for a good Soviet defection story. The month of July—the month of Nixon's détente talks with Brezhnev—had been studded with reminders of the Soviet regime's suppression of freedom. Americans were aware that even ballet stars had suffered. Only two weeks before Baryshnikov's defection the former Kirov dancers Valery Panov and his ballerina wife Galina Ragozina had finally been allowed to leave Russia for Israel. The story of their persecution by the Soviet authorities had been well documented in the newspapers, and personalities from the theater and dance worlds throughout the West had protested their plight. Two days after Misha's defection, American television screens had gone blank as Soviet authorities pulled the plugs on network news teams reporting from Moscow on Soviet dissidents. The anti-Soviet demonstrations during the Bolshoi's performances in London had helped publicize Soviet persecutions. Sakharov was on hunger strike. It all added up to a very unpleasant picture of life in the Soviet Union. Baryshnikov, people assumed, must have been driven by a terrible suffering to forsake his home.

Misha was careful to dispel myths about his treatment in the Soviet Union. In interview after interview he insisted that his decision to leave had been purely artistic; that except for creative freedom he'd been given everything he needed in Leningrad, that he'd never had any problem with the authorities, and that he'd never suffered any material or physical deprivation. If he was suffering, he said, it was only because he missed his home.

Misha could have said more about his problems with the Soviet ballet establishment—mainly about its politicization, its bureaucratic heavy-handedness, the way one was forced to cheat and lie and betray one's principals in order to succeed—and several years later he did. But for now he was being careful. He concentrated on the theme of homesickness, the divided soul. He was sacrificing his personal happiness, he stressed, for the sake of his art alone. Yet the press found it hard to let go of the notion of persecution. *Newsweek* described Baryshnikov as sitting restlessly through the August 12 interview, "his eyes and head impatiently scouring the room as if looking to escape." Kirkland, too, held onto the myth for as long as she could. She had no other way of explaining Baryshnikov's sullen moods.

Emotionally, it took Misha many months to adapt to life in the West. Americans sometimes find it hard to understand the pain of upheaval. By tradition, Americans value mobility and independence. Russia, on the other hand, is historically an insular country of rooted people. Besides, the summer of 1974 in New York was the first time that Mikhail Baryshnikov had ever been really alone. He had many new friends but few close friends—and for Misha it is only those friendships that have matured over time that really count. "You have to spend years with people before you can know them deep," he once said. There was nobody he could call if, late in the night, he needed to talk. He had trouble interpreting people's feelings and expectations.

Misha wasn't alone, he was lonely. He was surrounded by casual admirers. Not only was he a celebrity, he was also very popular among Americans because of his playfulness, his incredible impersonations, and his easy manner. But for a long time Misha felt most comfortable with fellow émigrés. He met the poet Joseph Brodsky after only a few weeks in the States, and they have remained close friends ever since. Dina Makarova, who had helped Misha as an interpreter at the time of his defection, became a constant companion in the first few months. She spoke for him, guided him, and propped him up socially. He needed it; he felt insecure in his new city.

Soon Misha met Remi Saunder, a cheerful, middle-aged

woman émigré who had helped many in their transition from Soviet to Western life. Saunder quickly became a mother figure to Misha. She, in turn, introduced him to other members of the Russian intelligentsia living in the West, including Rostropovich, the renowned cellist, and Alexander Galich, a dramatist and poet who had become something of a dissident star in the Soviet Union with his politically satirical songs. Like Misha, Rostropovich, Galich, and their wives were newly uprooted from their Russian soil. These friends, with whom he could discuss Russian literature, drink vodka, tell Russian jokes, and reminisce, became Misha's cocoon.

In Leningrad, rumors were circulating to the effect that Misha was miserable, that he was virtually begging for forgiveness on the steps of the Soviet embassy, that he wanted to go home. The rumors were persistent and believable enough to worry Misha's friends. Finally, Nina Alovert sent a telegram to Sacha Minz in New York, asking him to call. For over a week Sacha and Misha's calls were intercepted by an operator who insisted that nobody was home. Finally, having almost given up hope, they reached Alovert and Misha managed a brief, breathless conversation with a friend he could never hope to see. This was the first in a series of calls to Leningrad that helped assure Misha that he was neither forgotten nor despised for having left his friends. Through them, he later learned of Lapauri's death. Having been refused tours and other privileges, Misha's tour leader quickly drank himself into oblivion and was finally killed when he crashed his car into a tree.

The phone calls helped Misha, but he was still far from happy. He would retreat into an impenetrable world of his own. He was sad and jumpy. Most of all Misha needed to be settled, surrounded by his things. The luxury of his penthouse suite could not compensate for the lost comfort of familiar objects and places, his personal world. His friend, Brodsky once said that Misha's life had been made up of "a series of attachments to objects, to animals, to things which are less than human." He

missed his dog Foma and the streets and skies and waterways of
Leningrad. Misha hated the noise of New York. He missed
Leningrad's stillness, the elegant restrained quiet. No one raised
his voice there, no one pushed. In New York the pace was
frightening. It was ten times faster than in Leningrad.

Misha's notion of physical beauty was shaped by the perfect
harmony of streets like Rossi Street and by the delicacy of pastel
facades against a low, pale horizon. On the elegant Nevsky
Prospekt, the American Singer Building had been considered an
ugly incongruity. Now Misha walked in the dark and dirty can-
yons of Manhattan, where the horizon is lost, and the towers of
glass and steel rise so carelessly. It was all hard and raw and
brashly gleaming, absolutely unbeautiful. And yet, despite the
loneliness and disorientation, this new life was exciting. This
was the "beauty of ugliness."

Baryshnikov had defected in Canada but not to Canada. It
was America that had caught his imagination, or at least an idea
of America, the America of vulnerable antiheroes. As a kid,
Misha's America had been the cartoon land of Tarzan and fat
men with hydrogen bombs, gold coins, and big cigars. Then he
began to read Hemingway, Faulkner, Tennessee Williams, and
"the country finally started to materialize in my head somehow."
When Misha first met Brodsky, a few weeks after arriving in the
United States, Brodsky asked him how he felt when he walked
around the city streets. "I said that I felt I was growing up every
minute," says Misha. "I wanted to try everything."

In between workouts, rehearsals, and performances, Misha
soaked up American culture. He went out almost every night, to
parties, dinners, and especially to movies, musicals, and the theater. When he stayed home, he watched television. He learned
his new language through the media and movies, and his image
of America was formed by Broadway, the networks, and Hollywood—movies like *Chinatown, Butch Cassidy and the Sundance Kid,
American Grafitti,* and *The Sting* were showing that first summer in
New York. When, at the beginning of 1975, *The New York Times*

invited Misha to name some movies for its "Favorites pick their Favorites" feature, he answered with a strange blend of pure Americana and heavy European: including *The Seventh Seal, Snow White, Gone With the Wind, The Idiot, That's Entertainment,* and *Blazing Saddles.*

Nineteen seventy-four was the year of Watergate. News stories about Misha were half buried beneath accounts of the "plumbers' trials," and day by day the networks were broadcasting the Watergate congressional hearings. It was an intense period in America's self-definition. Years later, after another summer of congressional hearings, this time on "Irangate," Misha said, "I think a person should live where he wants to live, in a country whose politics he respects. . . . A lot of Americans have disagreed for years with American policy, but it's their country; it's their choice to fight it or leave it, you know? . . . I cannot imagine myself anywhere else, like it or not. It's incredible! This country spoils you."

Toward the end of August Misha returned to Canada briefly for a guest performance with the National Ballet. Gelsey took the opportunity to go to London, where she hoped to be fitted for new toe shoes. They had become quiet lovers with a language problem; Gelsey's attempt at a Russian language course hadn't helped. Their romance was, in her words, "a fitful routine of nocturnal visits," Misha arriving at her apartment late at night, "like an orphan looking for shelter," and leaving early in the morning.

Returning to New York, Baryshnikov and Kirkland finally began to rehearse for the coming season. Misha had chosen the ballets—Makarova's staging of the "Kingdom of the Shades" scene from *La Bayedere* and the *Don Quixote* pas de deux that he had danced so successfully with Makarova in early August, as well as the full-length *Coppelia* and Balanchine's *Theme and Variations,* both new to him. This was to be his first attempt at Balanchine and Kirkland's first experience with Russian story ballet. Both would be forced to make some difficult technical transitions; in effect, they would each have to train in each other's method. For the first few weeks Misha became Gelsey's teacher. Working with her daily in the studio, he tried to introduce her to the rigorous discipline of the Russian syllabus. But Kirkland's body couldn't take the strain to which Baryshnikov was accustomed. Nor could Misha seem to satisfy her intense, constant searching for fundamental insights into how and why he danced the way he did. To Misha, it was all automatic. He'd never had to analyze it. Kirkland began to feel that her approach to dance was not compatible with Baryshnikov's.

Nevertheless, the partnership developed, and along with it, so did the relationship. The routine began to vary. Gelsey would sometimes make the nocturnal visits to Misha's penthouse suite, arriving late and leaving early; they began to talk; and they went out together to gatherings of Misha's émigré and new American friends. As the summer drew to an end, they flew to Florida together for a weekend of fishing, horseback riding, and relaxation on Howard Gilman's estate. And yet, Misha was still suffering from homesickness. Without the distraction of work he sank into periods of melancholy and isolation.

In the first six months after his defection Baryshnikov learned, rehearsed, and performed seven new ballets, four of them modern. As he said at the time, perhaps he'd made the wrong decision in giving up his life at the Kirov—perhaps he would never get over it—but the only way for him to find that out was to dance. And that meant dancing often and in a range of styles. Misha's almost feverish activity was both the justification and the remedy for his self-exile. Like a child left alone in a candy store, he accepted every role offered to him. Some even suggested that, having been denied the right of refusal in the Soviet Union, Baryshnikov didn't know that in the West he could turn down offers to dance.

The American Ballet Theatre, meanwhile, was celebrating its best box office season ever. Baryshnikov's arrival seemed to mark a turning point in the company's difficult history. In October

Clive Barnes proclaimed the side effects of Baryshnikov's presence as beneficial; the competition was good for other male
dancers in the company, too, especially for Fernando Bujones,
who at twenty was the youngest principal dancer at ABT and
one who showed great promise. Bujones had recently been the
first American to win the gold medal at Varna—the same medal
Baryshnikov had won five years earlier. It was even suggested
that Bujones had the potential to develop into another Baryshnikov. Like a champion athlete, Misha was setting new standards
for American dancers.

After the ABT debut of Baryshnikov and Kirkland at the Kennedy Center in Washington, D.C., the press went wild. They
were the ABT's "golden children." The romantic partnership between these two attractive, young stars—a twenty-six-year-old
Russian defector and a twenty-one-year-old ballerina who had
defected from a rival company—appealed to gossip columnists
and critics alike. During curtain calls on stage and in interviews
they exuded innocent affection. "She is a diamond, well cut and
well polished, who could fit into any setting," said Misha. "Is she
cute? Oh, you mean beautiful?" Kirkland recounted how she had
first seen Baryshnikov in Leningrad: "He was the best dancer I
ever saw. Besides, he was cute. I can't say I didn't notice that."

The critics loved them. During performances, they detected a
special feeling flowing between the couple. He was serious, she
was playful. He was tender toward her, the perfect partner for
this fragile ballerina—"self-effacing, modest and utterly depend-
able," said Barnes. When they danced *La Fille Mal Gardée* in December, instead of the village idiot he had been with Makarova
in the same ballet only a few hours earlier, Misha became a
"romantic sweetheart" who responded to Kirkland's apparent fra-
gility with careful and protective partnering. They seemed to
have been dancing together for most of their young lives, said
Barnes, "as if they had grown up together. Perhaps they had."

In a sense, Barnes had hit upon a truth. Whether or not they
knew it, Misha and Gelsey were growing up together. Each hav-

ing left the companies that nurtured them through childhood, both had just left home. And together they were catapulted into the wide world of international stardom.

While the press effused, Baryshnikov and Kirkland played the loving couple. In Washington they shopped for cowboy hats and a new wardrobe for Misha, a more sophisticated, more hip wardrobe to suit his new life-style. Touring America they danced and partied and dined together and shared hotel rooms in city after unfamiliar city. By Christmas they were back in New York. The strain was showing. Kirkland had felt compelled to find an emotional key to the characters she was portraying in the story ballets, and she was all played out.

She and Baryshnikov had been performing the ballet *Coppelia;* Kirkland danced Swanhilda, a strong-willed peasant girl whose fiancé, Franz, is a simple flirt. Franz, underestimating Swanhilda, falls in love with a mechanical doll, Coppelia. Only when he realizes his own folly does he also understand that his beloved Swanhilda is much more than the pretty, silly "doll" he took her to be. Kirkland identified entirely with Swanhilda. Her aim during that period, she states in her autobiography, was to bring Misha to the point of realization that Franz reached in the ballet.

But Baryshnikov did not identify with Franz. He was fascinated by the more complex role of Doctor Coppelius, the darkly comic maker of dolls who had invented Franz's inanimate lover. In her review of *Coppelia* Arlene Croce wrote, "His acting tends to be a cover for his personality, not a revelation of it."

Baryshnikov was already growing restless with the heaviness of the traditional story ballets, the very tradition in which Kirkland was immersing herself so fully. Just before Christmas he made his debut as the Green Skater in Frederick Ashton's *Les Patineurs.* It was his first contemporary Western ballet, a light, breezy piece. Like Balanchine's *Theme and Variations,* for which he had been rehearsing with Kirkland, it called for pure, impersonal dancing. These ballets were vignettes. They contained no drama, message, or mime. Facial expression was out of place in them. "The characterization is in the role, it's in the steps," Misha wrote in *Baryshnikov at Work*. To succeed in these new roles Misha had to rethink everything he had learned in Russia. It was a great challenge, and one which interested him enormously. This was the promise of the year ahead. This was America.

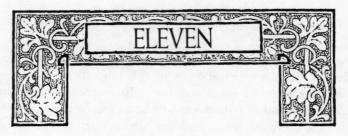

ELEVEN

Injury

 ON JANUARY 5, 1975, Baryshnikov partnered Natalia Makarova in *Giselle* and received yet more rave reviews for his riveting portrayal of Albrecht. That night Nureyev caused quite a stir in the theater lobby when he came to see the performance; later Baryshnikov, Nureyev, Makarova, Sacha Minz, and Valery Panov and Galina Ragozina gathered for a private party. It was the first complete gathering of the "Kirov contingent," a very Russian occasion.

On the ninth Misha made his debut in Roland Petit's 1946 ballet *Le Jeune Homme et la Mort* and immediately became ballet's most popular existential antihero. His versatility was astounding. In a matter of days he had switched not only style but persona. Gone was the dreamy Russian, the beautiful, grieving prince, the lovelorn young innocent living in a fairy-tale world of spirits and noble peasants, and even the boyish loner of the Green Skater. Gone, too, were the lavish scenery and ethereal ballerinas, the soft contours of traditional story ballet. Suddenly Baryshnikov was the lone young man of the blank generation.

He thrived on nihilism. He was pure, glaring, twentieth-century angst. Dressed in tight jeans and bare-chested, he smoked, he slouched, he angered, and, in the decadence of his cheap hotel room, he succumbed to death in the form of the female muse. With the brash blinking of neon lighting the act, he hanged himself.

Petit's off-beat choreography in *Le Jeune Homme* interested Misha, as did the experience of working closely with Petit in preparing the ballet. "He told me of that whole postwar neurosis; the exposed nerves, the 'agony of art,' the idea of living in 'the world as primitive fantasy,'" recalls Misha in *Baryshnikov at Work*. The choreography itself expressed the exposed nerves of which Petit spoke. It had Misha racing all over the stage, twisting and turning and spinning, leaping over tables and chairs, and practically climbing the walls. Moreover, the syncopation of steps and music demanded a certain amount of improvisation.

No one knew quite what to make of this new Baryshnikov. American critics felt that ABT had made a big mistake in reviving this ballet for Misha, which the company had dropped from its repertoire in 1951. The ballet, they complained, was not in good taste. In fact, it was affected, labored, vulgar, and outdated in its obsolete form of European existentialism—"a pathetic waste of his resources," one critic said. Yet this was Misha's first opportunity to dance in a ballet that lay entirely outside of the classical tradition and at the same time to pay homage to some of his biggest influences.

The ballet had been created in the 1940s by Petit—the Parisian choreographer with whom Misha had so wanted to work when they became friends in Leningrad in 1973—in collaboration with Jean Cocteau, who wrote the libretto. Misha had seen Cocteau's films in Leningrad and had been deeply impressed by them. The fact that the ballet was outrageously European didn't bother Misha; so was he. Cocteau's existentialist ideas appealed to Misha. He had met them before in Dostoevsky, one of his favorite authors. Here was the alienated individual, pitched against the hypocrisies of society and utterly alone in a godless, urban world, a poet inspired by dark passions, living recklessly according to pure, senseless desire and free to face death, the ultimate liberation. It has been said that whoever has read a lot of Dostoevsky cannot fail to be fascinated by suffering.

Cocteau's *jeune homme* was unmistakably modern. Fully responsible for himself and his actions, he was therefore tragically vulnerable. Misha had no problem interpreting this character, and the public sensed it. The image of Misha in blue jeans, a kind of psychological Misha, a hip, modern-day Hamlet of a Misha, quickly took over from that other very Russian Misha, the new boy in town.

In January Arlene Croce wrote: "It may be because of the unreasonable load of responsibility he has to carry, as much as his unaccustomed intensive performing schedule, that Baryshnikov is beginning to look a little tired." Misha had barely stopped to think. As the year began he had added yet another three ballets to his repertoire, two of which he had never before performed. Balanchine's *Theme and Variations*, which was totally unlike anything Baryshnikov had ever danced, had put enormous strain on his legs. "The first time I danced it," he says, "I thought my legs would drop off." He had been working relentlessly, touring all across America, and absorbing his new culture and new language, all the while involved in an increasingly strained relationship with Gelsey Kirkland. Misha was tired. He was tired even before he left New York on an extended foreign tour with Natalia Makarova.

Tours are exhausting for any performer. Touring means adapting to new environments and climates, impersonal hotel rooms, and constant traveling. It means never being able to fully relax and rarely being alone. For dancers, touring can be even more debilitating because of the difficulty of adapting to different stages, with their various surfaces and angles, plus the difficulty of staying in shape when they're miles away from the studio and their schedules are unsettled. An exhausted dancer runs an increased risk of injury; torn ligaments, tendonitis, and sprains are common symptoms of overwork. Mental strain makes for an even greater likelihood of injury.

One evening in February, during a performance of the full-length *Don Quixote* at the Sydney Opera House, Misha made a grande jeté across the stage, came down badly on his left leg, and felt his ankle turn under. "I could hear the sounds of bones crushing," he told *People* magazine in April, 1975.

Few in the audience were aware of it at first, but Misha had badly sprained his ankle. The pain was excruciating. Yet, incredibly, he danced through his injury right up until the final curtain. Unlike athletes, professional dancers do their best to conceal their pain. From the time they begin their training they learn how to mask the discomfort of even simple steps. Since ballet is the creation of illusions that can be ruined by the merest grimace of pain, dancing through injuries becomes second nature to professionals. But few dancers are professional enough to dance through the kind of pain that Misha felt when he landed from one of his highest jumps, or to come up with split-second changes in choreography. "I invented a step to keep going," Misha said later. By reversing the direction of a series of pirouettes, he managed to shift his weight onto his right leg. When the curtain fell for the second time and Misha dropped to the floor in a dead faint, Makarova screamed hysterically. The performance was over.

As soon as he was ready to travel, Misha returned on crutches to the peace and luxury of White Oak, Howard Gilman's Florida estate. He had strict instructions to rest and let his ankle heal completely before returning to his hectic schedule. This was his worst injury ever, probably because he had never danced so much before. He had never been under so much pressure. The number of roles he had taken on during his six months in the United States would have kept him busy for years at the Kirov.

There wasn't much to do at White Oak but relax and recuperate. He was surrounded by fifty-five-hundred acres of nature.

There were no reporters, no parties, no groupies, and no possibility of dancing. For five weeks Misha spent his days resting, swimming, reading, taking long, reflective walks through the woods, and fishing. He grew a beard and took riding lessons for the first time in his life. It was his first real break since the upheaval of the previous July, a break that his mind needed as much as his body did. Several injuries and seven whirlwind years later Misha commented, "It's very interesting psychologically—whether I use injuries to relieve the pressure."

Baryshnikov returned to New York during the first week in April and began to recondition himself through a diet and exercise program. In a sense, he felt renewed. He told an interviewer for *People* magazine that the shock of exile had worn off, but that he was still moody. He had lost a lot, he said. He missed even the beautiful air of Leningrad.

The honeymoon was fading for America and Baryshnikov. While Misha had become less of a mystery to the public, the critics, seeing him in modern ballets that didn't make the most of his Russian training, were becoming more critical. And after nine months in New York City, America was less of a fantasy for Misha, too. The dizzying excitement had worn off. The freedom of the press to delve into his private life had become a constant irritant, and he was disillusioned by his discovery that ballet in America was not as free and flourishing as he had once imagined. Many émigrés are surprised that in the richest country in the world, the arts have to struggle to survive. Misha was learning about the constraints imposed by the box office and about unprofessional training and presentation. Whatever had been the Kirov's failings, it had spared neither time nor funds in the preparation of its dancers and its ballets. There, he had never been expected to rehearse and perform on the same day. Misha was also learning about the ill-informed response of the public. It seemed as if America was more interested in what he did between performances than in the performances themselves.

Baryshnikov was quickly becoming a household name, a com-

modity. When *Time* and *Newsweek* both featured Misha as their
cover story in May 1975 he was packaged as a slightly reticent
playboy of the Western world, Russian to the core. He likes to
play, said *Time*, and he likes to party. But deep inside "he is
drawn to sad feelings, sad ballets." Baryshnikov was a romantic
hero.

Returning to the stage, Misha continued with his relentless
work schedule. Each day began with an intensively demanding
ninety-minute ballet class. It is a fact of ballet that even the
greatest dancers in the world must submit throughout their careers to the continual corrections of a daily class. If there was a
new ballet in preparation, which there nearly always was, Misha
would spend another six or seven hours in rehearsal. Unlike
most dancers, who walk through many of the ballet steps during
rehearsal, Misha always danced. On performance days he could
usually manage one hour of rest before curtain call. Misha gave
himself one free day a month—one day for reading, sleeping, or
fishing.

Soon Baryshnikov was on the move again, this time to Paris,
where he had been engaged to perform at the elegant Paris
Grand Opéra. Since his scheduled partner, the French ballerina
Noëlla Pontois, was unable to perform due to an injury, he
asked Kirkland to accompany him. In Paris, according to
Kirkland, she "skidded across a raked stage and back into
Misha's arms." Misha was used to the rather steep rake of the
Grand Opéra stage—after all, he had spent years in Leningrad
training in a studio and performing on a stage with a similar
slant. But for Kirkland, as for most American dancers, the stage
was very uncomfortable—so much so, in fact, that during one
performance she would have fallen into the audience had Misha
not pulled her back upstage by the back of her tutu.

Besides performance trips to Italy in the summer and to Ham-
burg in September, Misha spent the rest of 1975 growing rich
and restless. For a twenty-seven-year-old from Leningrad he was
earning a phenomenal sum with American Ballet Theatre—

three-thousand dollars per performance, for about one hundred performances a year. He spent the money on books, music, movies—anything to feed his appetite. He began to build up a substantial library of literature that had been unavailable or banned in the Soviet Union, and he read. He continued to go out whenever he had a free evening. He brooded. He was looking for something, for a new way of being a dancer.

Misha was beginning to feel a certain kind of drudgery at ABT. The same classics that he had left behind in Leningrad were performed here night after night, yet without the intense rigor that had marked the Kirov productions. Why had he left the Kirov? Not merely for star status and wealth, but for the challenges that he had seen through the window to the West. Yet in the West he had not yet danced a work choreographed specifically for him.

At ABT, resentments were building. The star status that Baryshnikov and Makarova were enjoying was attributed by some dancers to the fact that they were Russian. Russian defectors made such good public relations material for the companies that some members began to say they feared the next defection. There was even talk of a "Russian takeover." One soloist, quoted in Suzanne Gordon's *Off Balance*, recounted a dream she had in which the whole company was fired because the entire Bolshoi Ballet had decided to defect.

While Misha happily shared his Kirov technique and interpretations with his ABT colleagues, giving classes and offering advice, it was true that he was being favored with the most desirable roles and was getting all of the attention. Dancers like Cynthia Gregory and Ted Kivitt, who had worked hard for years and proven their worth at ABT, suddenly felt pushed out. And while Baryshnikov was lauded as a nice guy, Bujones was put down for being too cocky. Many ABT members felt that the company had come to rely almost exclusively on the star system instead of seriously trying to improve what had long been seen as ABT's main shortcoming: the lack of coaching and direction given to its dancers. And of course there was considerable dissatisfaction over wages. With Baryshnikov earning three-thousand dollars per performance, it seemed to soloists who had been working hard for ten years or so that their own earnings, around four hundred a week, were inequitable. Ever supportive of Baryshnikov, Lucia Chase responded by telling everyone, including the press, how wonderful it was to have such a generous, self-effacing dancer as Misha. ABT had just celebrated its thirty-fifth anniversary and the biggest box office season in the company's history.

Natalia Makarova, too, was voicing complaints. During an interview with John Gruen she gave her reasons for returning to join London's Royal Ballet as a permanent guest member—although she would continue to guest occasionally with ABT. Among the reasons, she mentioned her partner problems. She had been taking company class with Baryshnikov and Nureyev, and yet she had partner problems. Her dissatisfaction with Nureyev was well known; it dated back to an incident in Paris, when Nureyev had dropped her in a lift. But Baryshnikov? Wasn't he a perfect partner? "To be brutally honest about it," Makarova said, "I feel I give him more than he gives me." In *Giselle*, she said, she was always spontaneous in her emotional interpretation. Misha was always calculating. Makarova didn't dance with Baryshnikov during the 1975 summer season.

There were also problems between Baryshnikov and Kirkland over *Giselle*, which they were rehearsing together for the first time. Baryshnikov scarcely needed to prepare for his role. He had performed Albrecht so many times that he could dance it backward. But Giselle was a new role for Kirkland, and she wasn't about to settle for her partner's approach. She would not allow her Giselle to be a passive foil to Baryshnikov's tragic Albrecht. The tragedy is the heroine's—after all, she had been doubly betrayed by her lover and is doomed to die from the madness of a broken heart. Kirkland treasured her "mad scene"; she wanted nothing to distract from it.

She wanted Misha's Albrecht to achieve salvation through selfless love and repentance. But Misha was committed to his Albrecht, the innocent youth whose fatal flaw lies only in his intense love for Giselle. For Misha the tragedy was still his, and in recent performances the tragedy had grown to immense proportions. Misha had invented his own mad scene.

Kirkland was intent on resolving the differences between Misha and herself. She scheduled extra rehearsal time with Misha and took him to see her private teacher, Stanley Williams, at the New York City Ballet. Kirkland was famous for her obsessional perfectionism as a dancer. Now it was taking on another dimension. As the friction increased, America's favorite ballet partnership quickly degenerated into the sour remnant of a love affair. Perhaps Misha could envisage continuing the relationship on a purely professional level; Gelsey could not. Her emotional involvement in both the ballet and her partner was too absolute. On one occasion, angered by her repeated claims that his lifts in the second act were intentionally clumsy, Baryshnikov refused to dance with her. Only after Chase and a member of the teaching staff had intervened did he finally relent. In an interview a few weeks later, Kirkland publicly complained to critic Arlene Croce about those "chancy lifts."

Gennady Shmakov saw Baryshnikov and Kirkland perform *Giselle* at the Uris Theater in December of 1975, a year and a half since he had seen Misha's last Albrecht in Leningrad. Misha, he wrote, had distanced himself from the role; his "flawless mastery" was almost cold now, while Kirkland was brittle and brilliant. They were "two dissimilar beings, as if there were something essential that they hadn't said to each other in the first act, and as if that gap were now irreparable."

As far as the American ballet-going public was concerned, Baryshnikov was infallible. In the classical roles he was perfection. Yet Misha knew as well as Shmakov did that he was in danger of losing his spark. His career was soaring, but while he would always claim that dancing was just a job for him, he wanted to

be more than the greatest professional dancer in the world.
Baryshnikov was on display as one of ABT's "three Russians." He
was getting tired of all the talk about how successful he was.
"Listen," Baryshnikov once said, "the only advantage of success
is that you have another choice for another time."

Misha's "other choice" was Twyla Tharp. He had met her at
the Spoleto Festival of Two Worlds in Italy, where her new work
Ocean's Motion was being performed. *Ocean's Motion* was typically
Tharpian, a pop-art piece set to music by Chuck Berry. It was
an older work, *The 100s,* that caught Misha's attention. Watching
the performance, he began to understand Tharp's style and knew
that this was what he wanted: "It was so unexpected and mar-
velous that I was swept off my feet." Here was a truly American
dance, a twentieth-century, New-World dance. It was pure
Manhattan—wry, fast, funky, smart showbiz, and Misha loved
it. At first he thought one would probably have to be American
to do it. Misha felt that Tharp's original blend of classical ballet,
jazz, tap, and social dancing must require a special technique.

Baryshnikov had faced the challenge of Balanchine; he had
been preparing two works created by Michel Fokine for Nijinsky; and he had been dancing a modernistic work, *Shadowplay,*
by Anthony Tudor. Every one of these ballets challenged him
with new techniques and new approaches to characterization.
And at Spoleto he had premiered John Butler's *Medea,* the first
work created for him since his arrival in the West. He liked its
immediacy, the "charged, electric" feeling of the ballet, and he
had quickly mastered the pelvic contractions and the sharp
edginess of the work's Grahamlike technique. But in watching
Tharp, Misha finally saw his real challenge. It would also be a
big risk.

TWELVE

The Turning Point

 IN 1975, WHEN Twyla Tharp made her choreographic debut at Spoleto, she was considered one of the more controversial choreographers, or "dancemakers," in modern dance. She was also as American as they come. "She grew up in California where she spent much time riding in cars and listening to the radio," reads one account of her youth.

A thirty-three-year-old experimentalist who had studied with and broken away from both Martha Graham and Merce Cunningham, Tharp went in for tacky effects, popular music, fast, distorted steps, and gestures derived from American social life. There was a funny kind of flippancy that set her apart from her more serious contemporaries. Yet Tharp was serious. To the discerning eye, the cheeky humor of her work was a surface that concealed a perfectly crafted, highly structured dance. "The most important thing about Twyla's work is that it is very controlled and classical in intent," Baryshnikov wrote.

Twyla Tharp's work used and satirized the ballet tradition, but it was not a part of it, either classical or modern. It was modern dance, and modern dance in the seventies was still a different world altogether. It was avant-garde. Tharp had her own small company which had performed in gymnasiums, galleries, churches, and even once on the great lawn in Central Park. In 1973 she choreographed two pieces for the Robert Joffrey Ballet of New York—*Deuce Coupe*, set to music by the Beach Boys, and *As Time Goes By*, a restrained yet witty look at the conventions of ballet style, set to music by Haydn. With these two works Tharp became something of a celebrity.

In 1975 the directors of ABT were looking around for a new ballet that would show off Baryshnikov's comic talents. Just a couple of months before Spoleto they'd seen him in his revival of *Vestris*, the seven-minute solo that Yacobson had choreographed for Misha for the 1969 Moscow competition. To the American public *Vestris* revealed a new Baryshnikov. They'd seen him in love and they'd seen him anguished, but they had no idea of his true range. In *Vestris* he was really funny, a great mimic. Who else could have done justice to this witty mime sequence inspired by Marcel Marceau? In seven one-minute vignettes he went through seven changes of personality, from old man to coquette, to preacher, to praying woman, to the great Vestris himself, then to laughing drunken man, and finally to dying old man. Lucia Chase knew that finding the right comic role for Misha would make both him and the public very happy.

At the same time that she was looking for Misha's new ballet, Chase was considering commissioning a ballet from Tharp. Yet the idea of putting Tharp and Baryshnikov together never crossed her mind. After all, Baryshnikov was a great classical dancer and Tharp was a newcomer to the more rarified world of ballet. She was pop. Many in the ballet world considered her work glib entertainment. "She gives people what they want," was a frequent criticism. Tharp was risky business for a perfect classical ballet star like Baryshnikov.

It took the festival at Spoleto to bring the dancer and the

dancemaker together. "If they had not met at that particular
time," says Chase, "Ballet Theatre would still have added a
Tharp ballet to its repertoire and would eventually have produced a comic ballet for Baryshnikov by another choreographer,
but in neither case would the result have resembled *Push Comes to
Shove*." As far as Misha was concerned, Tharp was no risk. He
wanted to work with her. From his perspective he wouldn't be
much of a dancer if he didn't.

Push Comes to Shove was Tharp's response to Baryshnikov. She
built the dance around his personality. Like Yacobson, Tharp
saw the clown in Misha—his delight in sly impersonations, his
facility for absurd gestures and physical foolery—and the role
she developed for him gave that comic talent full range. He was
the bebopper, the man-about-town in a derby hat, the rough-
neck, the street crazy, and the nice guy, all in swift succession,
to a score that merged jazzy, upbeat ragtime by Joseph Lamb
with a piece by Haydn. The ragtime was, as Misha describes it,
Tharp's "calling card" to her new audience. It was her pro-
nouncement of her own all-American tradition, her parentage.

But this was not Misha's parentage, and Tharp realized how
much the dancer would have to learn. It wasn't just the off-
balance positions that were new to him, but also the entirely
American gestures and ways of moving—"even the way he puts
his foot into the floor or the way he shifts his weight," Tharp
told *The New York Times* in October, 1975. She had developed a
whole new way of dancing based on American vernacular
culture, and here was a Russian classical ballet dancer trying to
master it. "I always had the feeling in the beginning that I was
out in a boat that had no sail, doing forbidden things," wrote
Misha in *Baryshnikov at Work*.

Tharp and Baryshnikov worked painstakingly in the studio,
learning and building and polishing, and hour by hour their respect for each other blossomed. Baryshnikov was overwhelmed
by Tharp's intricate craftsmanship as much as by her incredible
sensitivity to the music. And Tharp was amazed at how Barysh-

nikov adapted so openly to the unfamiliar. It was a slow process, "hours and hours of very technical rehearsals, repetition over and over again," Misha wrote. He had never met such disciplined perfectionism, and it suited him. "To work with a choreographer is a unique experience," wrote Misha in connection with *Push Comes to Shove*, "a cross between the perfect vacation and being in church."

Push Comes to Shove was a smash hit. It was as if the stage had been opened up to joyful riot. Tharp had created a ballet that poked gentle fun at the world of classical ballet—Misha's world. All of the affectations, the squabblings, and the competitive attitudes were there. She'd choreographed a solo for Misha that in the space of a few frenetic minutes made witty reference to practically every major classical ballet in history. For the finale, derby hats went flying like champagne corks and the cast returned for final bows styled on the bows of certain star dancers.

Despite his initial difficulties in rehearsal Misha was the uncontested star of the production. In fact, although an understudy had been prepared for the role, ABT decided that it should be exclusively Baryshnikov's. If he was unable to dance because of illness or injury, the performance would have to be canceled. This was an exceptional decision at ABT, and it was due entirely to audience demand. There was simply no substitute for Misha in this role.

Twyla Tharp's *Push Comes to Shove* marked a turning point in the evolution of American ballet. Companies like ABT were beginning to feel increasingly secure in staging the more experimental and sometimes more popular works that were being created by America's modern dancemakers. In a way, this was the changing of the guard. Baryshnikov and a young choreographer had made their imprint on an evolving dance form, claiming ballet for their own generation. The years ahead would see a vital cross-pollination between the different dance traditions, attracting a brand-new, young audience. For this, Misha was largely responsible.

In an essay written shortly after the opening night of *Push Comes to Shove*, Lucia Chase wrote that ABT "had been instrumental in enabling Misha Baryshnikov to realize a cherished ambition—that of exploring the new territories being opened up by American choreographers. That evening alone would have convinced me that my thirty years as co-director of Ballet Theatre, with all its headaches, had been worthwhile."

Chase's headaches were lighter at the beginning of 1976 than they had been for a long time. ABT was in good shape financially after several good seasons with Russian stars drawing in the crowds. The company was even considering buying a theater, an old Oscar Hammerstein theater full of red plush, gilt roses, and chandeliers, an intimate gem with a huge stage. The theater had not been used since the Depression. An atmosphere of "empty beer bottles and lost coffee cups" hung over the place, as Clive Barnes described it, but with about a million dollars in renovations it could be perfect. The idea of having a permanent home had long been a dream for this sprawling, nomadic troupe.

Nevertheless, there were headaches. Cynthia Gregory had suddenly resigned from the company at the end of December 1975, unhappy, apparently, with the roles and number of performances she and other American dancers had been given in the winter season. There were just too many principal dancers sharing too few choreographic opportunities. By then, according to the press, the company was "wrecked with dissention" brought about by management's favoring of Russian stars.

To add to this, it looked as if Gelsey Kirkland was falling apart. She'd refused to partner Baryshnikov in Tharp's ballet because, as she said, "I had no inclination toward that brand of entertainment," and then she'd made herself sick to justify missing what everyone, especially Baryshnikov, said was the chance of a lifetime. Kirkland had always been prone to compulsive behavior—since her visit to Russia she had repeatedly starved herself—and she was doing it again, but now her dancing was

Six months after defecting from the Soviet Union, a homesick Misha celebrates freedom and reunion with former Kirov stars Rudolf Nureyev, Valery Panov, and his wife Galina Ragozina. This private party was the first meeting in the West of the "Kirov Contingent." While the Soviet stars partied in New York, a joke circulating in Leningrad dubbed the depleted Kirov Ballet as the "Kirov *Corps* (corpse) *de* Ballet." *Photo by Frank Teti/Neal Peters Collection*

Misha with friend and former Kirov colleague Natalia Makarova, at an opening party in May 1976 for New York's fashionable restaurant, Regine's. Accompanying them was choreographer Jerome Robbins, who had been rehearsing the two stars in *Other Dances*, a pas de deux he created especially for them.
Photo by Frank Teti/Neal Peters Collection

Misha arrives with actress Shirley MacLaine for the premiere of *The Turning Point* on November 14, 1977, at the Coronet Theater. The movie thrust Baryshnikov into a new world of superstardom, and earned him an Oscar nomination for best supporting actor in his role as Yuri, the flirtatious Russian ballet dancer. *Photo by Tim Boxer/Pictorial Parade*

Eliot Feld rehearses Misha in *Santa Fe Saga*, a romping solo created by Feld for Baryshnikov which featured the Russian dancer in a series of archetypal American poses—from heroic cowboy to Indian scout. *Santa Fe Saga* was the last guest performance Misha gave before becoming a "first-amongst-equals" at the New York City Ballet in 1978. *Photo by Lois Greenfield*

Baryshnikov and Gelsey Kirkland dance in American Ballet Theatre's production of Balanchine's *Theme and Variations*, April 1978. When Misha first danced this piece in 1976—at the time the only Balanchine ballet in the ABT repertoire—he called it the most difficult and most pleasurable choreography he had ever performed. By the spring of 1978, Misha had stunned the dance world with his decision to defect from ABT to Balanchine's New York City Ballet. *Theme and Variations* was to be his last dance with Kirkland before leaving the company. *Photo by Lois Greenfield*

Baryshnikov and Jessica Lange attend an American Film Institute tribute to John Huston at the Beverly Hilton in March, 1983. *Photo by Russell Turiak*

(inset) Misha and daughter Alexandra, aged 4½ in November 1985. Since Misha and Alexandra's mother Jessica Lange parted ways in 1983, Alexandra has lived most of the time with Lange and actor-playwright Sam Shepard. But she still visits her father in New York, and remains the light of his life. *Photo by Danny Chen/Star File*

Misha and his childhood hero, James Cagney, attend the premiere of *That Championship Season* in New York City, December 1982. As a boy growing up in Latvia, Misha spent hours standing on line to get a ticket for a Cagney movie. Later, when the two finally met in 1978, they became good friends. Misha was a pall-bearer at Cagney's funeral in 1986.
Photo by Russell Turiak

Misha holds a tap shoe, "King of Tap" Gregory Hines holds a ballet slipper, and director Taylor Hackford brings them together at the Bistro in Beverly Hills in March 1984, at a reception to publicize their then untitled movie. During the location filming of the movie, *White Nights*, Misha came closer to his homeland than he had for ten years. "I'm still surprised I got into it," said a physically and emotionally exhausted Misha after the movie's release in November 1985. *Photo by Frank Edwards,* © *Fotos International*

Baryshnikov in the 1986 ABT production of Karole Armitage's controversial ballet *The Mollino Room*. The ballet cast Misha as the lonely outsider, unable to connect with the dancing couples around him. His spiky, disjointed movements led *Time* magazine to proclaim, "Baryshnikov Goes Punk."   *Photo by Lois Greenfield*

[right] Baryshnikov as Tony Sergeyev, artistic director and lead dancer of a touring ballet company, and ABT's Alessandra Ferri, as leading ballerina and Tony's one-time lover Francesca, rehearsing as Albrecht and Giselle in the 1987 movie *Dancers*. The movie, directed by Herbert Ross and featuring Baryshnikov's staging of the ballet *Giselle*, portrays Misha as a modern-day parallel to the jaded playboy Count Albrecht, in a story that parallels not only the ballet's story, but also the stories that have developed around the life of Mikhail Baryshnikov.

Mikhail Baryshnikov and choreographer Twyla Tharp at a benefit in May 1988 for the Twyla Tharp Dance Foundation, held at the Silvercup Studios in Long Island City, New York. Dance patrons paid $1,000 each to be videotaped in a specially choreographed piece. Ever since Twyla Tharp created the smash-hit *Push Comes to Shove* for Misha in 1976, the collaboration between dancemaker and dancer has produced a large and immensely popular body of work.
Photo by Tom Gates/Pictorial Parade

Misha in his apartment in Leningrad, 1974.   *Photo by Nina Alovert*

(inset) With his dog Foma.   *Photo by Nina Alovert*

IN THE SOVIET UNION:

In a Soviet television production of Hemingway's *The Sun Also Rises,* Misha plays a straight dramatic role.   *Photo by Nina Alovert*

The Creation of the World.   Photo by Nina Alovert

[inset] Playing with Foma at his Leningrad dacha.   Photo by Nina Alovert

Daphne and Chloë.   *Photo by Nina Alovert*

Rehearsing American Ballet Theatre production of *Cinderella*.
Photo by Nina Alovert

Three Virgins and the Devil, American Ballet Theatre.　*Photo by Nina Alovert*

With Zizi JeanMarie in *Carmen*, Paris.   *Photo by Nina Alovert*

(inset) The Queen of Spades, Roland Petit Company, performed in Paris.
Photo by Nina Alovert

Apollo, American Ballet Theatre. *Photo by Nina Alovert*

ABT rehearsal.   *Photo by Nina Alovert*

suffering and the press was beginning to refer to her "emotional turbulence." Tales of Baryshnikov's romantic relationships with members of the ABT corps and of Kirkland's broken heart made intriguing copy. It was Kirkland who told a reporter, "He goes through everybody, he doesn't miss anyone." Ballet Theatre had been thriving on the scandal. But now Lucia Chase had a problem: should she schedule Kirkland to dance and risk having to cancel, or should she not schedule her and run the risk of Kirkland breaking down completely from lack of confidence? Kirkland was, as dancer Ivan Nagy puts it, "a genius living on the edge of a razor blade."

And of course there were always the day-to-day problems that nobody outside the company—not even the board of trustees or the "friends of ABT"—could be aware of. There were little squabbles inside the ABT "family" to deal with, there were ballerinas throwing tantrums over their costumes, and there were continual scheduling problems.

Even Baryshnikov gave Chase problems. Makarova referred to his "artistic promiscuity." There were complaints that he was too busy to give himself to any one choreographer. Tharp had been complaining that while she generally spent five hundred hours of rehearsal time preparing a new dance, with Misha she could schedule only about seventy. Other choreographers with whom Misha had been working voiced the same complaint; he was grabbing every new opportunity that came his way and was spreading himself too thin. "He's a very, very busy boy," said Anthony Tudor, "I do hope he'll grow out of it."

Misha was busy. Like a kid, he could not get over how popular he was, how much everyone wanted him. He just could not keep up with the demand. "Should I dance five *Giselles* traveling around Germany," he joked, "or should I go to Monte Carlo to dance two galas for Prince Ranier? What a dilemma!"

After two years in New York Baryshnikov had performed thirty roles, many of them new, and had traveled all over the world. At the Kirov he had learned about twenty roles in seven years. He was making up for lost time, breaking the mold of his Kirov training. At times it was confusing; Misha was living in a whirlwind. In May 1976 he made his debut as a guest with Alvin Ailey's Dance Theater, performing in a gala with Judith Jamison in *Pas de Duke*, to music by Duke Ellington. Baryshnikov and Ailey had been planning this for almost two years—there just hadn't been time until now. Here was another new experience: for the first time in his life Misha wore jazz shoes instead of ballet slippers and learned a "whole different world of movement." "'Don't look at me, don't look at me,' I said at the first rehearsals," remembers Misha. "I looked like a cow on ice."

At the same time, Baryshnikov was rehearsing with Makarova for another new pas de deux, *Other Dances*, by choreographer Jerome Robbins—also for a gala, and yet another whole different world of movement. Misha went from one rehearsal to another until he could hardly remember what he was dancing where. Although Misha felt more comfortable with his jazz movements by the premiere of *Pas de Duke*, he was still nervous. He didn't want to make a fool of himself. He did lose the orchestra at one point during the performance but says "it was great fun, really *fun* to dance."

Misha was also busy becoming a movie star, although in 1976 he had no idea that Herbert Ross's movie *The Turning Point* would make him more famous than he already was. After all, he was not an actor, and his part in the movie was relatively small. As he liked to insist, the script had no scenes in which he appeared with the real stars of the movie, Anne Bancroft and Shirley Mac-Laine. How could he be a movie star? He could scarcely speak intelligible English. He was just Yuri, a Russian dancer with the American Ballet Company (ABC), modeled on ABT, who toys with the affections of a couple of ballerinas, including the love-struck young Emilia.

The story of Yuri and Emilia was secondary to the main story of two middle-aged women, Emma (Bancroft), an aging prima ballerina with the ABC, and Deedee (MacLaine), once an ABC dancer and friend of Emma, now a wife and mother of three who runs a ballet school with her husband, also a former dancer, in Oklahoma. Twenty years earlier, Emma had landed the part that shot her to stardom. Deedee had wanted the part, too, but she was pregnant and Emma convinced her to continue the pregnancy and get married. Deedee has regretted her choice to this day. Emilia, Deedee's daughter and Emma's goddaughter, is accepted into the ABC and, with the fading Emma as her coach, finds herself an overnight star in a new, modern ballet. Along the way she falls in love with Yuri, is seduced and partnered by him, and is then abandoned for a young Giselle. But she has replaced her godmother as the company's shining light, and Emma is left to bravely contemplate a life without dance or glory.

The Turning Point was the original conception of Herbert Ross and his wife, the movie's executive producer, Nora Kaye. Both former dancers, they had been wanting to do a ballet movie for years. Kaye was a charter member and prima ballerina of ABT until she left at the age of forty-one. Ross was a dancer there, too, until he turned to choreography. He made his first feature, *Goodbye Mr. Chips*, in 1969 at the age of forty-two, and followed with movies like *The Owl and the Pussycat* and *Funny Lady*. When Baryshnikov arrived in New York and shook up the ballet world, Ross and Kaye decided it was time for their ballet movie. They wanted to make a mature film that portrayed the real life of the ballet dancer—all of the backstage nitty-gritty, the sore feet, the hard work, and the petty intrigues. By revealing dancers as normal people with normal problems, they hoped to open up ballet to an even wider audience. Ross made his case to producer Alan Ladd, using ballet attendance statistics as supporting evidence. Finally Ladd agreed. He had been credited for backing films that portrayed women in meaningful roles, and he thought Bancroft and MacLaine as Emma and Deedee would be interesting characters. He wasn't so sure about the ballet angle.

The central story of *The Turning Point* was based on real life. As a young ballerina at ABT Nora Kaye knew a dancer who, like Deedee, had left the company to get married and raise a family. The oldest of her children, Leslie Browne—Kaye's real-life seventeen-year-old goddaughter—had recently been accepted into the corps of the New York City Ballet. Screenwriter Arthur Laurents developed the story, inventing the romantic subplots. By November 1975 the treatment was ready and a black-tie dinner, peppered with Hollywood personalities, was held in Los Angeles to promote the project. ABT was in town at the time, performing at the Dorothy Chandler Pavilion; the dinner was timed to begin right after the performance.

The idea was to have Baryshnikov and Kirkland as Yuri and Emilia. In fact, Yuri's part was conceived and written expressly for Misha. Laurents cleverly structured the screenplay to give the two nonactors a minimum number of scenes and not too much to say. With Baryshnikov and Kirkland in supporting roles they could afford to worry less about the box office—after all, how many people would want to see a ballet film starring two middle-aged women? But they couldn't count on Kirkland to dance—she was just too fragile now—so they decided to use Leslie Browne as dance-in for Kirkland. Like Emma, Kaye wanted to give her goddaughter a break, and Balanchine agreed to give her time off from the company in order to shoot. While Ross, Kaye, and Laurents developed the treatment and the script, Ross kept on feeding Ladd statistics of ballet box office grosses.

When the scripts arrived in the early summer of 1976 Misha was immersed in his new ballets. Kirkland was dancing, too, sometimes with Misha, sometimes not. They had established a distance from each other. Kirkland claims to have been resistant to the idea of Hollywood from the start, but having turned down the hit *Push Comes to Shove*, she accepted the movie. The more involved she became, the more she wished she had turned it down. She disliked the script immediately. She couldn't identify with Emilia, who she considered empty-headed. She was concerned about the love scene—she didn't want the whole world to see the scars from her silicone implantation surgery. Worst of all, she worried that the public would jump to the conclusion that the story was really about Misha and herself— which, of course, it was, with undertones of Leslie Browne and her family.

When it came to rehearsals Kirkland tried to revise Emilia, apparently in her own image; however, she says, "every time I introduced an idea about the character to Herb, drawing from my own experience, and winning his tentative approval, he turned to Nora [Kaye] and hit a stone wall." Kirkland's response was to start starving herself again, using every known prescription for weight loss including vomiting, thyroid pills, enemas, and celery juice. She'd been on a downward spiral anyway.

Apparently, Misha was comfortable with the script but not with his acting. Ross, who has a reputation for drawing good performances out of nonactors, read through the screenplay once with Misha, then put him in front of the camera, and said, "Do you know the lines?" "I said yes," recalls Misha. "And he said, 'Just do it, don't worry.' Later, he said, 'I want you to do it the way you are; I don't want you to act—be yourself. You're a Russian dancer from the moon!'"

Sergei Yursky had told Misha the same thing and more, years before in Leningrad, when he directed him as the matador Pedro in *Fiesta*. "For an actor the path to the spirit of a character always lies in the body, in movement," Yursky once wrote. *The Turning Point* was Baryshnikov's first English-speaking movie role, but it was not his first movie acting experience. He had undoubtedly learned a considerable amount about film acting from Yursky, one of the most outstanding actors in the Soviet Union.

Misha's first complaint about movie acting has always been that he can't stand the waiting. Yet the most difficult thing, according to Misha, is to be yourself when the person you're supposed to be talking to is behind the camera and the film is rolling. "I felt very shaky," Misha told John Gruen. "What was difficult was not knowing the intensity with which to speak. . . . And I was worried about my facial expressions—that sort of thing." He couldn't tell what was good and what wasn't, which worried him more than anything. Misha's main problem with *The Turning Point* was his accent. As Ross said in an interview with Stephen Farber, "Misha can act. But he has a speech problem. The accent is thick. And when he's nervous, his English goes completely, and there's a long pause while he translates it into Russian."

Misha was painfully self-conscious about his accent. When he felt insecure he would run his palms over the sides of his head and fluff his words, then run off the set, embarrassed: "I am sorry, my mouse is full of garbage."

Most grueling of all was the filming of the dance sequences. The crew often worked from six in the morning until nine at night, and the dancers had to be warmed up and ready to go the whole time. Misha was well aware that this would be the first time that millions of people would see him dance, and he wanted them to see him at his best. He now admits that the pieces he danced in the film were not very demanding—"all bravura," he says.

Shortly before shooting began, the studio panicked. They were very unsure about investing so much money in what was still considered an offbeat movie. Ross had to tighten the budget considerably; script changes continued throughout the filming. They would have to shoot the whole thing in twelve weeks. Then, days before shooting was set to begin on Emilia's scenes, Ross decided not to use Kirkland. She was ill. In the preceding months her weight had dropped from ninety-five to eighty-one pounds. According to Kirkland, Ross and Kaye had suggested a health farm, but she had refused and had continued her self-destructive cycle of bingeing and dieting. She was entertaining notions of her own death—or madness.

Without delay, Ross and Kaye replaced Kirkland with Browne. "We had tested Leslie on camera, and she had exactly the kind of look we wanted," said Ross. What they wanted was the very young, very innocent look of a girl who would fall for a Russian heartbreaker. Browne was only seventeen, and by the time she stepped in front of the camera she looked very much like Gelsey Kirkland.

Events had given an ironic twist to the story. As Emilia, a character based loosely on herself, Browne was suddenly a star, and in large part this was due to her godmother. Asked how he enjoyed working with Browne, Misha answered that she was young, pretty, nice, and alive, which "helps when you do a love scene." She was an interesting dancer, too. In fact, he says he enjoyed dancing with all of the ballerinas in the movie.

Browne was slightly in awe of Misha; she was particularly nervous about the intimate bedroom scene. Ross took pains to ease the pressure. To give the actors a sense of privacy he closed the shoot to everybody but the technicians. The next day, Browne showed up looking much happier. "But," she said, "Misha was trembling all through it."

When Misha first saw rushes from *The Turning Point* he was shocked. He thought he looked terrible. Ross tried to persuade him that he looked very good, and that all actors hate themselves when they first see rushes. When everyone else on the set started telling him how good he was, Misha thought they were talking about his dancing. He preferred to think about the thing he did best. Nevertheless, he didn't discount the idea of trying again. His acting part was tiny, he told an interviewer, as it should be for a first movie. Next time perhaps there would be more.

The Turning Point was released in the fall of 1977 to mixed reviews. Some critics felt the movie was entertaining but hackneyed in its conception and development. Beneath its serious intent it tasted a little like a soap opera. It had been promoted as a ballet film but was instead a backstage film, complete with bitchiness, glamor, and romantic intrigue. The dancing, complained some critics, served no dramatic function in the story. "The method is that of show-biz not art," said Vincent Canby in *The New York Times*. Other critics loved it. Here at last was a mature, sensitive movie about universal emotions. Here was middle age treated with respect; here was the blood, sweat, and tears of the ballet world. But in every review, good and bad, the real star of the movie was Mikhail Baryshnikov. He was credited as much for his excellent, low-key acting ability as he was for his stupendous dancing. "Ross's biggest weakness is that he doesn't trust the camera enough. If he did, it would take him right to Baryshnikov," said Pauline Kael in the *New Yorker*.

As the reviews piled up and the press besieged him, Misha was ambivalent. He continued to talk about his dancing and to wax modest about his acting. He spoke about his fascination with movies and with the whole filmmaking process, but he was evasive when it came to commenting on *The Turning Point*. He was only "man from street," he would say, implying that he had had nothing to do with the film. In fact, Misha was reportedly horrified when he saw what they had done to the movie in the editing room. He couldn't accept the fact that the actor has no control over the end product. He especially disliked what they had done to Yuri. Baryshnikov felt they had used him unfairly for their own ends, playing on his press image. He had never expected Yuri to be such a Casanova, and he repeatedly vowed never to take on another movie. Shortly afterward, when Ross invited Baryshnikov to star in a movie he wanted to make about Nijinsky, Misha refused. He decided to make his own Nijinsky movie but then became so busy that he had to drop the idea several months into the planning stage.

Despite Misha's misgivings and the many criticisms leveled against the movie, *Variety* correctly predicted a huge box office success for *The Turning Point*. Across America people flocked to see not only MacLaine and Bancroft but also Baryshnikov. They had read about him and seen him pictured with one or another beautiful woman, and here was their first chance to see him, almost in the flesh. At the same time, people were interested in catching a glimpse of the nuts and bolts behind ballet's ethereal stage presence. They'd already had a taste of it from Gelsey Kirkland, whose behind-the-scenes troubles made for tasty gossip.

The Turning Point did give millions of people a glimpse at the real life of ballet dancers. But it was a small glimpse. In classroom scenes shot at the ABT school with two ABT coaches they witnessed the intense discipline and incredibly hard work that dancers must endure. They saw the dispassionate preparation that goes into one of the most romantic performance arts. They may have been surprised to see that stars like Baryshnikov take daily classes with members of the corps. They caught a glimpse of the ballerinas' sore, misshapen feet and the lonely, narrow life of hotel rooms and mirrored studio walls.

Through characters closely resembling actual ABT personalities people were introduced to the political hierarchy of ballet: director, stars, established choreographers, young choreographers, soloists, and, right at the bottom, the corps members. And they were given a larger look at the tragedy of the aging ballet star who must finally, at the peak of her mental maturity, give up the life for which she has forsaken everything else and help some naive young dancer replace her in the limelight. This theme of aging, of change and continuity in ballet, with Misha's Yuri belonging to the new generation, came through strongly. So, too, did the image of Yuri/Baryshnikov as a captivating Russian heartthrob, an inconsiderate seducer of young ballerinas.

Early in 1978 Misha was nominated for an Oscar for best supporting actor, and the press followed him everywhere. Now he wasn't just a ballet star, he was a movie star, "one of the most electrifying newcomers on film." While Misha went back to ballet and prepared his own staging of *The Nutcracker*—another new experience for him—America read about his private life: his passion for spicy Chinese food, his favorite drinks, his dislike of sweets, his incredible earnings, his taste in women. "His blue-grey eyes have an 'over-ripe' look and hint at unreported night-time activities," said *New York* magazine on May 8, 1978.

Misha, now the highest-paid dancer in the world, professed to prefer privacy while letting just enough of himself escape. "I adore women," he said. "I just don't know why my private life has become some sort of symbol. I'm not the first straight dancer or the last." Perhaps the root of the matter was that Misha could not resist the challenge of making pretty girls fall in love with him. He liked to be liked, and he loved to be loved, but even more than that he believed in the inspirational power of desire, which he says is "what all poetry is about."

Baryshnikov kept insisting that on the whole he was too busy and too tired to lead the wild life people were imagining. "Listen," he told a reporter. "It's silly. I take a girl out to dinner once and—big story. It is overdone, this reputation." But reporters kept digging for romance. He was reported to be romantically involved with Leslie Browne. Dancers on the set of *The Turning Point* remarked on how Misha had been "unusually attentive and considerate" to her, "something more than brotherly." Another dancer said he'd flirted with all of the ballerinas on the set. Whether or not he was sensitive to the possibility that the real-life Browne may have fallen for the real-life Baryshnikov, he quickly put an end to rumors of their romance. At a party thrown in honor of the two as stars of *The Turning Point*, Misha arrived with an unexpected date, Jessica Lange.

THIRTEEN

Affairs of
the Heart

IT MAY HAVE seemed inevitable to some. Misha was on the verge of becoming a hot new movie idol, and he had found himself a Hollywood starlet to partner—for a while, anyway. Everyone knew that his relationships didn't last. That was all part of the excitement his personality generated. He was an "eligible bachelor." At the moment he was immersed in Hollywood, so he belonged to Jessica Lange, who played the dumb blonde in that most Hollywood of productions, *King Kong*.

That's how it looked in the gossip columns. In fact, Baryshnikov was busy making balletic inroads and Lange was no Hollywood starlet. She was a serious, private beauty from the Midwest who had studied painting at the University of Minnesota and mime in Paris before ending up in New York and having her life interrupted by a year-long Hollywood nightmare.

When Milos Forman introduced Baryshnikov to Lange at a Hollywood party, Lange had just finished playing damsel in distress to an imaginary forty-foot ape on a Hollywood lot. "She's

King Kong's girlfriend," Misha was told when he asked who she was, to which he reportedly replied, "Who's King Kong? Can I meet him?"

"King Kong's girlfriend" was the tag that Lange was desperately trying to shake. She wasn't interested in being a starlet, and she wasn't a dumb blond cover girl, as Hollywood's publicity machine was trying to portray her. Only a year earlier she'd been living in New York City, taking acting lessons, doing some experimental theater work in SoHo, and trying to make ends meet by waitressing at a writers' bar in Greenwich Village. Occasional modeling jobs had brought in extra cash. When the offer came to do a screen test for Dino De Laurentiis's *King Kong* she'd accepted; her main thought was that it was a free trip, she'd never been to Los Angeles, and she might be able to hook up with her sister in San Diego. Within a week she was signed and they were shooting a $25-million movie that was destined to flop. As she put it later, the movie ended up being a joke, and that made her a joke, too.

Lange met Baryshnikov at a difficult time in her life. Demoralized but wiser after the *King Kong* experience, she was certain she'd taken a wrong road and had to start back at the beginning. She cared too much about her work to let her career fall to pieces. Lange knew what was right and she knew how to look out for herself. She was, as Jack Nicholson once put it, "a delicate young fawn crossed with a Buick."

According to Baryshnikov it was love at first sight: "we were very attracted to each other." Lange turned her back on Hollywood and moved back to New York. She had no agent and no answering service. She wasn't looking for another break. She'd lost her job and her apartment, but she was still under contract to De Laurentiis, and that paid her salary while she returned to acting class and began researching the life of Frances Farmer, the legendary actress in whom Lange had developed an intense interest.

The last thing Jessica wanted was to ride along on Misha's

star. "It angers me when I run into women who are totally sub-
missive, completely dependent," Lange once said. "What angers
me more are men who like that kind of woman." Jessica had
been alone enough and had been down to her last quarter often
enough to know that ultimately she took care of herself. She had
her life—including a house in Wisconsin and a husband, the
Spanish photographer Paco Grande, whom she'd married as a
teenager and from whom she'd recently separated—and Baryshnikov had his.

In the beginning, Baryshnikov was the busy one. He was
learning fewer new roles, but he was involved in another challenge: his first attempt at staging a production. Nureyev had
staged ballets for several companies, Makarova had staged *La
Bayadere* for ABT, and now Baryshnikov was going to try his
hand at *The Nutcracker*. ABT hoped to profit from having this
favorite Christmas classic in their repertoire.

Misha admitted to being "nervous as a cat" about the whole
project. He insisted that he was not making his debut as a choreographer, he was merely restaging a ballet that had been done
over the years in many different forms. Nevertheless, his job was
difficult and demanding. Besides developing his own interpretation of the story of Clara and her uncle Drosselmeyer and en-
visaging it in balletic terms, he wanted to expand his own role,
the Nutcracker Prince. Baryshnikov had to choreograph all of
the new material and then mobilize the forces that would turn
his idea into reality. "You pick the dancers, you pick the de-
signer, you pick the form," said Misha. It was like a second
apprenticeship in theatrical directing—his first taste had been at
the Kirov, with the "creative evening" disaster. Later Misha
would point to this period as the one in which he first learned
about responsibility. At times it was a burden, made all the more
difficult by the problem he had communicating in English.

Taking cues from previous productions and also from his own
understanding of Tchaikovsky's score, Misha interpreted the
ballet as an adult story, with Clara's dream symbolizing a rite of

passage from childhood to womanhood. He had Gelsey Kirkland in mind for the leading role. Misha brought out the darker aspects of the tale and developed the role of the prince for himself with some brilliant new choreography. As a special Freudian touch he characterized the mice as male guests at the party.

When Baryshnikov's *Nutcracker* opened in December 1976 it fulfilled all of ABT's commercial dreams. It was an immediate popular success. Even Misha's friends in faraway Leningrad heard about his triumph. His dancing in the role of the prince was, of course, miraculous as ever, his choreography was intensely musical, and the snow scenes were as magical as a Leningrad winter. The critical response—that the production wasn't that original, and that there was a slight lack of clarity in the interpretation— was almost beside the point. As Clive Barnes pointed out, ABT didn't need this ballet in a repertoire already overloaded with comfortable classics, and the only artistic purpose it could possibly serve was to keep the company financially afloat. Misha's *Nutcracker* could hardly fail to triumph as a popularization of ballet.

Ballet was quickly capturing the imagination of America, and everyone knew that Baryshnikov was responsible. Attendance at ballet performances had tripled since Misha first brought the house down in New York in 1974. The release of *The Turning Point* emphasized the trend. In one Chicago ballet school, student applications, especially from boys, were said to have suddenly increased by twenty-five percent after the movie was shown locally. It was just as one of the characters in *The Turning Point* said of the dancer Yuri: "He's going to make it respectable for American boys to become ballet dancers." One month later, American ballet and male dancers got another popular boost with the well-timed national television broadcast of Baryshnikov's *Nutcracker*.

The production, underwritten by IBM, was filmed in Canada during one hectic week in October. It was difficult for everybody. The stage was small, and scenes had to be shot out of order, take after take, until every detail was correct. Baryshnikov's old friend Sasha Minz played Drosselmeyer and Kirkland, who had danced various roles in Balanchine's *Nutcracker* since her first role as the angel at the age of ten, danced the part of Clara.

Kirkland had missed the opening season of the ballet, having very suddenly decided on an operation to remove the scars from her previous silicone implantation and its removal. Then, during a long and arduous ABT summer tour that took the company all over Europe, her relationship with Baryshnikov had taken a turn for the worse—at one point, the two had to be forcibly separated from a fight. But gradually the sparks had subsided and Kirkland seemed to be regaining her emotional balance. She had found a new boyfriend in ABT soloist Richard Schafer, and that helped her deal with the knowledge of Baryshnikov's attachment to Jessica Lange.

Nevertheless, when it came to filming, Kirkland once again disagreed with Baryshnikov's interpretation. Like Tanya Koltsova before her, she was unable to separate the emotional relationship from the working relationship. Gelsey expressed her confusion by quibbling and throwing tantrums, making rehearsals more difficult than ever. She had her own idea about Clara. She said she had found in this character a childhood of the imagination which she herself had missed by immersing herself in ballet—as a child she'd had aspirations, not dreams—and she would not allow Misha to take that vision of childhood away from her. She was determined that Clara should retain her essential innocence as she passed into womanhood.

Despite all of her intransigence and her tantrums, Kirkland became the perfect Clara, a believable twelve-year-old girl with an enduring dream of beauty and perfection. The role gave her the opportunity and the incentive to regain her stature as one of America's leading ballerinas; as *Time* magazine put it, this was her first triumph "after a period of physical and emotional travail." And with Kirkland as its star, *The Nutcracker* became, for all of America, Baryshnikov's *Nutcracker*.

Mikhail Baryshnikov and ballet were by now inextricably linked in the American consciousness. The more popular Misha became as a personality, the more popular ballet became, and the more popular ballet became, the more Misha's face and name appeared in the pages of the popular press. Now that face and name were paired with Jessica Lange's. Lange was learning to deal with the fact that Baryshnikov was a star and she was a nobody and, more difficult still, that his work was the talk of the town while hers may as well not have existed. "One night at dinner with what was the Greek aristocracy," Lange told Julia Cameron in an interview for *American Film* magazine, "this man leaned across me and said to Misha, 'I see you travel with your secretary.'" For Lange it was a choice between giving Baryshnikov up and getting on with her own life, or enjoying him while he was around and shutting the rest out. She wasn't ready to give him up.

Misha and Jessica had a lot in common. Both were intensely serious about their work without being obsessional. They sought perfection but knew there were other things in life. Baryshnikov has often said that ballet dancers miss so much because of their exhausting schedules. While many dancers hardly seemed to notice the world around them, Baryshnikov always tried to keep in touch. When he and Lange were together they took pleasure in shared interests—visits to museums and galleries, movies, concerts, meals in Chinatown.

They both loved dogs. Misha shared the one-bedroom apartment he rented on Park Avenue with a large, faithful poodle named La Goulue, after the famous cancan dancer painted by Toulouse-Lautrec. He once tried to explain his feeling for animals: "animals give you love and a kind of devotion that has no equal in the human world." Lange had the same way of avoiding commitments, of keeping a slight distance between herself and all but the closest of her friends. Even more than Baryshnikov, she tried to keep a part of herself private. "I always felt there was something I didn't know about her," said Lange's good friend and one-time lover, director Bob Fosse. People had said the same of Baryshnikov. Also, Lange was restless, always searching. She'd moved twenty-five times in the last fifteen years.

But right now, Baryshnikov was more ambitious than Lange. From the start she knew that he was moving along at high speed while she was standing still. He had his life; he would come and go. He had an insatiable appetite for new experiences, which, combined with ABT's grueling touring schedule, kept him moving. In the past year alone he had danced all over Europe on an ABT tour that relied heavily on him. He had also performed as a guest with the Royal Ballet in London, partnering Natalia Makarova in *Giselle* and *Sacre du Printemps*, a striking, modern ballet by Glen Tetley that created in the audience an uproar unseen for twenty-five years. He had worked hard with Makarova, helping her reconstruct the *Romeo and Juliet* that Igor Tchernichov had choreographed for them in Leningrad. He was still a very busy boy.

Now Misha was going to produce his own staging of the full-length *Don Quixote* for ABT. Again, many stagings had been made of the ballet since it was first created by Marius Petipa in 1869, including one by Nureyev in the sixties. Nevertheless, it was a natural choice for Misha's second production. *Don Quixote* was one of the few ballets in which he had performed regularly during his Kirov years, and in Leningrad he had been regarded as the best Basil ever.

Misha called *Don Quixote* "a crazy Russian salad" of a ballet. Don Quixote and Sancho Panza were barely featured in the original, slightly farcical story of the barber Basil's love affair with the mischievous innkeeper's daughter, Kitri—a story that had never made much sense to anyone. In fact, the ballet was a wonderful excuse for virtuoso dancing and funny pantomime. Criticized for his original version of *Don Quixote* when it first appeared in the nineteenth century, Petipa had replied that he was merely trying to please his Maryinsky audience. Misha, trained to the peak of professionalism in the same Maryinsky, was also trying to please his audience.

Having successfully staged *The Nutcracker*, Misha was much more comfortable in his role when it came to *Don Quixote*. He knew what he wanted, and he was convinced that this time around he would be able to have plenty of fun with it. Without making substantial alterations to the choreography as it existed at the Kirov, Misha wanted to create a pop version of *Don Quixote*, a nonstop, fast-paced feast of acrobatic dance and gags that would keep his audience laughing and clapping from beginning to end. Baryshnikov's version of *Don Quixote* was to be a kind of Broadway ballet that would hold the attention of a broad American public; after all, *The Turning Point* was quickly sweeping across America and the next season would almost certainly bring an audience that was entirely new to ballet. Misha called his vision "classical vaudeville," an Americanized Russian salad.

With the help of Elena Tchernichova, who had just arrived in the States from the Kirov, Baryshnikov rehearsed his cast through the winter of 1977. A cast of seventy dancers plus three sets of principal dancers had to be taught their roles. The company was on the road again, and so work on the new ballet had to be squeezed into a busy tour and performance schedule. They rehearsed in studios all across America, from Washington to Los Angeles to Chicago. It was a long, hard process.

To create his vision of classical vaudeville, Misha decided to cut the ballet from the traditional four acts to three, to do away with much of the mime, which had slowed down the traditional version, and to reorganize the order of unlikely events so that the story made more sense dramatically. For the whole thing to work, the dancing had to be perfectly timed and executed, and what remained of the mime had to be doubly effective. Misha worked and worked with his cast, demanding their best. He was uncompromising and unrelenting. By the time the curtain rose on the first night, about three hundred hours of rehearsal time had been invested.

Baryshnikov had chosen Kirkland to partner his Basil in the leading ballerina role of Kitri. Gelsey tried to pull out, claiming that she was totally unsuited for this joyous, fiery part with its devilish leaps. But when Misha told her she would do fine, Gelsey accepted it as a personal challenge. She took private lessons in Spanish character dance and femininity—how to unfold and hold a fan, how to ruffle a skirt, how to walk provocatively, and so on. "A Spanish woman is always in control with a man," her Spanish coach told her. Kirkland also scheduled secret rehearsals while Baryshnikov was out of town, it was the only way she could find to get some of her own ideas into the production.

After seventeen weeks of touring and rehearsals, followed by a spate of production meetings that often dragged on until the early morning hours, Misha's *Don Quixote* made its debut at the Kennedy Center in Washington, D.C., on March 23, 1978. The cast had managed a first run-through of the ballet only two days earlier. Misha had scarcely found time to catch his breath, and now he had to satisfy a hungry audience with a high-energy performance as Basil. Misha was the choreographer, the star, the virtuoso, and the screen idol rolled into one tired body. And he knew he was on display.

At about midnight on the night before the opening, lines had begun to form for standing-room-only tickets. At one thousand dollars a box and one hundred dollars a seat for the gala performance, the auditorium was completely sold out. In the audience were President and Mrs. Jimmy Carter, who had reportedly become Baryshnikov fans after seeing *The Turning Point*. As the show ended, the stars received a standing ovation and the flowers came flying to land at their feet on the stage while Kirkland, fully in control, presented Baryshnikov with a Spanish fan. "Showbiz Pizzazz," "Cheeky, Innovative," "Exhilarating," read the reviews the next day. Misha had succeeded. He had created a Broadway ballet for America. With *Don Quixote* the ballet boom was at its peak.

But Misha was tired. He was exhausted from the effort of it all and he was sick of being on display. At midnight, as Baryshnikov and Kirkland made their entrance into the candlelit atrium of the Kennedy Center, wealthy patrons of the dance engulfed them with congratulations while the press took notes on Misha's black suede jacket and boots and the guest list of Washington dignitaries. The evening's fiasco centered on the fact that at an earlier buffet supper, provisions of steak tartare, miniquiches, ice, and vodka had run out. Leaving Gelsey to sip Virgin Marys, Misha made a quick escape to his dressing room, where he flopped into a chair and despondently eyed the huge straw donkey that was occupying center place.

During the rehearsals for *Don Quixote* a strange piece of news had arrived from Leningrad concerning Yuri Soloviev: he had been found dead at his dacha. When they discovered him he was lying in bed with the blankets pulled up over his body and a bullet in his temple. He was still holding his hunting rifle in his hand. Soloviev was thirty-seven years old. People had always drawn comparisons between Baryshnikov and Soloviev, and now Misha's friends in Leningrad were saying that had Baryshnikov not left, he, too, probably would have been driven to suicide. Perhaps the news jogged Misha's memory. Perhaps it caused him to think about the frustrations that four years ago had made him do the unthinkable.

Misha often considered the opinion of his friends and fans back in Leningrad as they watched his progress in the West. He felt that he had somehow betrayed them in leaving Russia, and that he had to justify that betrayal by living up to their expectations of him. In general, he cared what his friends thought almost more than what the critics thought. There were one or two people close to him, people not involved in dance or show business, whose opinions he valued above his own. Like his faraway

Leningrad friends, they helped him keep a perspective on what he was doing. Misha was grown up now, but he still felt insecure in his opinions. Some choices were too difficult to face unless he had advice that he could trust. How else, when he was so caught up in the whirl of work and celebrity, could he remember to stand back and look at his life?

FOURTEEN

Mr. Baryshnikov Meets Mr. B

MISHA HAD BEEN taking stock. He had always believed that the essence of great dancing was ultimately to "dance the truth the way you know how," and he was beginning to feel that he was dancing a lie. He had left Leningrad in part so that he could dance more frequently, and that he certainly had accomplished. But primarily he had left to escape the endless repetition of Kirov classics, the same frustrations that had driven Soloviev to his death. Now ABT was becoming more conservative every season for the sake of a commercial success that seemed designed to capitalize on Misha's star image. He was being hailed for performances in those same classics from which he had thought to escape.

Of course, *Don Quixote* was a huge success. When ABT opened its New York spring season at the Metropolitan Opera House a record fifty-two-thousand dollar's worth of tickets were sold in the first day. Thousands of dollars had been spent on the production. In fact, not long afterward Cynthia Gregory—who had returned to ABT a year after her resignation over the favoring of Russian stars—resigned again, complaining that while the company was willing to invest a fortune on Baryshnikov's *Don Quixote* (about two-hundred-thousand dollars on costumes and sets alone), it would not invest the money to hire the Rumanian dancer who she had requested as a partner. Her complaints were buried in the media blitz that followed *Don Quixote. Time* magazine ran a cover story on the ballet on May 1, 1978, labeling Baryshnikov the "John Travolta of High Culture" and Kirkland "one of the most electric actresses now working on any stage."

Misha knew there were other things in dance beyond his *Don Quixote,* never mind how many thousands had been spent or made on it or how much bite-sized steak tartare had been devoured on opening night. There was something really great, something that stood apart almost majestically from the grabbag showbiz world of box office ballet, something for which Misha had been yearning for years, even before he had first entertained the thought of flying through the forbidden window to the West. Misha had never forgotten the guest performance of Balanchine's New York City Ballet at the Kirov Theater in 1972, when he sat awestruck in the audience while Gelsey Kirkland and the rest of the company performed the purest choreography he had ever seen.

"I need the choreography more than it needs me," Misha had told a critic back in 1976 when he danced in *Theme and Variations,* the only Balanchine ballet in the ABT repertoire. It was the most difficult ballet he had ever performed, and yet it was one that had given him enormous physical pleasure. As far as Misha was concerned, Balanchine was the master. He was the greatest choreographer of the twentieth century, and next to his creative genius even the greatest dancer in the world was nothing. In his fifty years as a choreographer Balanchine had created a new world of dance. It was he who had truly built an American ballet on the foundations of the rigorous Leningrad classicism.

Balanchine was a Russian who had managed to tap the

American dream by defining a form of ballet inspired by American tastes while retaining the elegance of old Leningrad. His neoclassical style was quick, precise, agile, and pure of body. He stripped away the storytelling and dramatic mime that were so much a part of the Russian sensibility and welded movement to music. He was the most musical of choreographers—his collaborations with Stravinsky were groundbreaking—and the most physically demanding. He took the strict, classical steps of the Russian school and set them off balance, one after another, without respite. He was an archetypal modern with all of the grace of old Europe. He was a creator not only of dances but also of dancers, and in this he was a god. "Mr. B" reigned supreme over his company and his school, and his word was final. Balanchine's dancers were his instruments, his raw material.

"I can't ask him to use me," Misha once said of Balanchine. "He doesn't want guest artists. He believes that dancers like me should dance what the public expects. But every dancer wants to dance exactly what the public doesn't expect." Misha wanted to ask but could not—he always said one could not ask to work with choreographers one admired. One must wait to be invited. But Balanchine wasn't inviting. In fact, he had barely acknowledged Misha's existence. He had seen Misha dance when *The Turning Point* was screened for him; "He has good feet," the master said. Balanchine didn't have stars. Dedication to dance, he felt, could only be corrupted by star status, money, and all that went with it. City Ballet was like a church, and its dancers were expected to serve the choreography. When Nureyev, soon after his defection in 1961, asked to join Balanchine's company, Mr. B told him that when he got tired of playing the prince he could come back and ask again. Misha couldn't stand the thought of such a reproof from Balanchine. There he was at Lincoln Center, only yards away from Balanchine's New York State Theater, and yet he could not ask him.

Nor could he stand to remain at ABT. It was more than just boredom with the classical roles; he reportedly told Kirkland that he could no longer deal with ABT's artistic directorship and vacuous star system. He had made up his mind to leave. For a period of time he investigated the possibility of creating his own small traveling troupe of six or seven dancers. He went so far as to gather considerable financial support and discuss possible engagements with directors of European companies.

Yet the more he thought about it, the more Misha knew that all he really wanted was to go to Balanchine and be an instrument in the master's hands. It would almost be like going back home. He wanted not only the challenging choreography, but also the structure, the intense discipline, the strict standards, and the purity of style that he had known at the Kirov. Besides, both he and Balanchine knew that the New York City Ballet was in fact the direct descendant of the Leningrad school. As such, it was his natural home and the only real justification for his having left the Kirov.

Misha was beginning to think that the time was now or never. Balanchine was seventy and, from what Misha had heard, his health was beginning to fail. In mid-March Balanchine had suffered a mild heart attack which had kept him hospitalized for two weeks. And Misha himself was no longer a young dancer. "Slowly I realized that I would never forgive myself if I did not try," Baryshnikov later told reporters. "I am thirty, with a few years left. If he said, 'You are not right in some way, physically,' I would go through a terrible depression, but I could stand it."

Misha couldn't bring himself to step across the plaza, walk into Balanchine's office, and ask him directly. Instead he decided to use the connections he had with the City Ballet. One of these was Peter Martins, who had never made the break from the City Ballet that he and Kirkland had planned. Martins had been telling Baryshnikov to approach Balanchine for years, ever since their first meeting in Leningrad. But Baryshnikov had achieved celebrity status instead of joining Balanchine's church, while Martins had thrived under Balanchine's guidance. Martins was disappointed in Misha, and he told him so. He didn't believe in the celebrity life Misha was leading because, as he said, "all you do is go somewhere and dance something you've done before, and then you put the money in the bank." Now that Baryshnikov had established his star status in America he was coming around to Martins's way of thinking.

Misha's other City Ballet connection was Jerome Robbins, Balanchine's associate ballet master and choreographer and a man for whom Baryshnikov had great fondness and respect. Robbins was a giant of dance in his own right, having created such Broadway hits as *West Side Story* and *Fiddler on the Roof* before returning to ballet and Balanchine. In 1976 Robbins had choreographed the plotless ballet *Other Dances* specifically for Baryshnikov and Natalia Makarova. Working with him had been a "complete revelation" for Misha and he longed to work with him again.

Misha let Robbins and Martins know that he would be more than happy to trade in stardom and the ABT for the chance to work with Balanchine. Then, early one April morning, he had a phone call. "I think we ought to talk," offered Balanchine. Misha was ready. He went directly to Balanchine's apartment, where the old man was still resting after his heart attack. Within half an hour, speaking in Russian over a cup of tea, these two giants of American ballet had agreed on an arrangement.

On April 26 Misha announced to the press that he would join Balanchine's New York City Ballet in the summer as a regular member and at regular pay. The ballet world was incredulous. How could Baryshnikov forsake everything—money, power, and stardom—for a seven-hundred-dollar-a-week job in which he couldn't possibly excel as he did in his classical roles? Misha responded with evident glee: "Some people here are skeptical, but my Russian friends will understand at once and rejoice." When Balanchine was asked for a statement later he answered simply, "We have so much to do and so many people sick, it's good to have someone healthy."

Just as four years ago Misha had assured the lawyer Jim Peterson that he really wanted to defect and that he was aware of its implications, now he assured the world that he knew what his defection to the City Ballet would mean. "I never called myself a star," he said. "I'm a dancer." Classical ballet, like the traditional novel, was built around heroes and heroines; as a principal dancer he had naturally been the hero. But unlike many ballet stars, Baryshnikov was prepared to be just one dancer in a modern ensemble. "For Balanchine and Robbins," he said, "I would be one of ten!" He was also prepared to risk failing to master Balanchine's style. What mattered was the challenge. Misha would be taking a drastic cut in salary, but he didn't need money. In his four years with ABT he'd earned more than two-hundred-thousand dollars a year, much more than he needed.

On May 18 Baryshnikov gave his last performance with ABT at the Metropolitan Opera House, dancing Robbins's *Other Dances* and everyone's favorite Misha role, Tharp's *Push Comes to Shove*. After the performance the audience showed its appreciation with eighteen minutes of heartfelt applause. Fans rushed down the aisles and threw flowers. Happy, Baryshnikov waved back to his waving fans.

His four years with ABT, he said, had gone by in a flash. And yes, he had changed. Like everyone else, he'd been running around at a speed he had once thought impossible. He had become, if not an American, a true New Yorker. Like a chameleon he had changed his skin, and now he spoke not in the high-minded tones of Leningrad Russian but in pure New York slang. "I just turned around now to ask for some Sweet 'n Low—that's already the stamp of America on me, isn't it?" As if to drive the point home before joining Balanchine, Misha had one last fling as a guest star in the romping *Santa Fe Saga*, a solo choreographed by Eliot Feld for Baryshnikov which featured the dancer in a series of archetypal American frontier poses: the Mexican nodding under his sombrero, the heroic cowboy, the Indian scout, the proud bandit. It was great fun, and once again Misha showed his chameleonlike powers of self-transformation. It was

"as if he'd been born on the Rio Grande," said one reviewer.
Now he was ready to drop everything else and immerse himself
in a master-student relationship.

Skeptical critics estimated that Baryshnikov would last six
months to a year with Balanchine. After that, they guessed, he
would give up and return to classical ballet. They pointed out
that two male ABT stars, Ivan Nagy and Eric Bruhn, had made
the same move ten and twenty years ago, and both had been
forced to quit within a few months. Many believed that Baryshnikov and Balanchine would inevitably step on each other's egos,
and they doubted that Misha could deal with not being a star.
Besides, they pointed out, Balanchine did not choreograph virtuoso parts for male dancers. "Dance is woman," he had always
insisted; the male dancer was primarily a consort. According to
a popular joke in ballet circles at the time, Misha was switching
companies because, having flirted his way through all of the ballerinas at ABT, he was looking for a new source for his amorous
impulses.

There were also rumors that Gelsey Kirkland would follow
Baryshnikov back to her old City Ballet home. But Gelsey had
no such intentions. One evening, before he had made his press
announcement, Misha had called Gelsey to tell her of his plans.
"His last words," she recalls in her autobiography, "buzzed in my
ear like a winged insect: 'Maybe someday I come back, Gelsey.'"
Kirkland sadly resigned herself to his absence and soon had a
new partner at ABT, a talented young dancer named Patrick
Bissell.

In June Misha traveled to the New York City Ballet's traditional summer home in Saratoga Springs—a town more famous
for its sparkling spring water and racehorses than for dance. It
was from there that Kirkland had called him just after his defection in Canada, as he waited to begin his life in America. And it
was there, in the quiet, relaxed setting of an informal arts center
with its great lawn and 5,500-seat pavilion, that Baryshnikov
now began a new life with Balanchine.

Though busy, things were quiet for a while and the atmosphere was happy. Misha rehearsed with the company, Balanchine was pleased with his progress, and everyone seemed to enjoy Misha's presence. He was learning a brand-new style, which opened up his insecurities and endeared him to his new colleagues. Jacques D'Amboise eagerly taught Misha his own part in *Stars and Stripes*, created for him by Balanchine twenty years earlier. According to Peter Martins, the celebrity dancer never set himself apart from the company, never behaved like a superstar. Even so, some of the younger dancers couldn't help seeing Baryshnikov as a star. They would watch him in rehearsal with keen interest, and as soon as he left the rehearsal room they would try out some of the new moves they had just witnessed. But there was none of the jealousy and strife that had dampened spirits at ABT. "We know we're all unique in Balanchine's eyes," said ballerina Patricia McBride.

In their free time Baryshnikov and Balanchine often got together at the country cottage that was Balanchine's home during the summer season. He loved to cook, and he would invite Misha for meals. Together they would sit under a large oak tree in front of the cottage and talk in Russian about their homeland, America, food, women, and, sometimes, dance. Before the morning rehearsal Misha could sometimes find time to go fishing in a nearby stream. Gradually Baryshnikov and Balanchine developed a warm friendship—Misha hadn't had such a relationship with a ballet master since his teacher Pushkin had died six years earlier.

On the afternoon of July 7, 1978 Misha made his debut with New York City Ballet. His matinee appearance in Saratoga Springs was entirely unannounced and miraculously inconspicuous. In fact, had some of Baryshnikov's chic admirers been there they would have thought the whole affair somewhat ridiculous, right there in the thick of middle-American life. For as Misha waited to go on stage, Ronald MacDonald, the fast-food clown, introduced the performance to an audience consisting mainly of mothers and children who filled the seats and spread out over the lawn with their sodas and their picnic baskets, unaware that they were about to see a performance by the great Mikhail Baryshnikov.

Misha danced with his new partner, Patricia McBride, in Balanchine's speeded-up version of *Coppelia,* one of the few classic ballets in the City Ballet repertoire. Balanchine had apparently included it in 1974 as a way of involving children from the school in performances. Besides the experience it would provide budding dancers, he reportedly thought that if every child in the ballet were to bring parents, brothers, and sisters, then *Coppelia* would have an automatic audience.

Following his debut, people flocked to Saratoga Springs to catch a glimpse of Baryshnikov. Suddenly the peace was broken. In an effort to maintain privacy for the company Balanchine changed rehearsal times in the outdoor theater; he changed performance schedules and put "to be announced" on all cast lists; and he closed off, locked, and guarded all of the backstage areas. But the word was out. Saratoga Springs was overrun by fans, hawkers of souvenir programs could be heard calling "Get your Baryshnikov photos here," and the box office hardly knew what had hit it. Balanchine was innundated with calls requesting "casting information" from directors in every theater in every city in which the company was scheduled to perform.

After a visit to Denmark with the City Ballet Misha returned to New York and set to work learning new ballets and perfecting a new style. It was demanding work. He had to retrain his body in the Balanchine style, a style that even younger dancers have found overly taxing. Whereas in classical ballet there are always a few preparatory steps leading up to a difficult leap or turn, in Balanchine's ballets there are none. The body twists and jumps from one position to another without any transition. The distorted body positions, performed in very quick succession, are painfully difficult, especially for a classically trained dancer.

The warmup period in Balanchine's daily class was too short

for Misha and he worried that he would dangerously strain his muscles. Instead Stanley Williams's advanced class, which he took with Peter Martins, followed at noon. The two dancers would take their place at the barre every day and, in the kind of friendly competition that Misha had engaged in with the young Godunov in Riga and with Panov at the Kirov, they would leap and turn across the floor, to the envy of the younger dancers. Martins was thriving in Baryshnikov's company. He had begun to grow bored with dancing, and it was a real challenge for him to compete with a dancer like Baryshnikov.

Even more important, according to Martins's girlfriend, Heather Watts, Martins now had a friend in the company. This was probably important for both dancers. Baryshnikov had a way of breaking through Martins's very cool, cerebral seriousness. In class and later, in the dressing room they shared, he would imitate Martins's stern postures, the almost heroic jut of his jaw, his tall, Danish nobility. And Martins gave Baryshnikov all of the support he needed. He, too, had experienced the problems that Misha was now having as he adapted to a new way of dancing. It had taken Martins three years of pain and exasperation.

Baryshnikov made his New York City debut with the City Ballet in November, dancing Balanchine's lightning-speed *Rubies*. The occasion was unusually chic—suddenly it seemed that Balanchine's State Theater was the place to be seen; even *Women's Wear Daily* had proclaimed the City Ballet and Baryshnikov, the current ballet "ins." Critically, Baryshnikov's performance received a measured response. While some were amazed at the ease with which he was adapting, others felt that he had not yet mastered Balanchine. He looked strangely old-fashioned and out of place. Balanchine's idea of impersonal dancing was based on what he saw as the special charm of American dancers, the mechanical quality of the chorus line. Misha had not yet learned to express himself purely through movement, without the play of emotions. He was still a Russian dancer.

Balanchine's health was deteriorating. His periods of intense fatigue had returned and were growing worse, and his work was suffering. When he was able to coach Baryshnikov he worked in astonishing detail, but much of the time Baryshnikov worked without the benefit of Balanchine's help. Moreover, he was not producing new ballets, so Baryshnikov was deprived of the honor and experience for which he must have been hoping above all else: a Balanchine work created specifically for him. As his health declined, Balanchine relied more and more on Jerome Robbins to fulfill his obligations to the company. In January 1979 Misha made his debut in the first work choreographed for him in his seven months with the City Ballet, Robbins's *Four Seasons*.

The new ballet was the first City Ballet production to make full use of Baryshnikov's virtuosity. Robbins gave him huge, dazzling leaps and lifts, turns, pirouettes, and *fouettés*, all performed at incredible speed. Arlene Croce called his performance a "one-man revolution"; Hubert Saal said the choreography was so ambitious that it threatened Baryshnikov with "instant curvature of the spine." During one *fouetté*, from which he rose in the air turning and landed, still turning like a helicopter, the faces of Baryshnikov's manager and publicity agent apparently turned ashen with fright. Misha was incredible but he no longer had a boy's flexibility, and they thought that perhaps he was being a little reckless.

In February 1979 Misha entertained at court, making his White House debut at the invitation of President Jimmy Carter, who had instituted a series of Sunday afternoon cultural events in the East Room. The event was to be televised by PBS on Easter Sunday, giving America the opportunity to see Baryshnikov perform Balanchine. The challenge lay mainly in negotiating the small stage, which took up half of the East Room and was not designed for dance performances. A reproduction of the stage was made and installed at the New York State Theater so that Baryshnikov, Heather Watts, and Patricia McBride could rehearse for a month before the February 25 performance. One week before the event the East Room was blocked off for full rehearsals.

The program of selections from Balanchine and Robbins had been rechoreographed on a diagonal orientation, so as to avoid a large chandelier that hung treacherously low over the stage. Even so, Misha's high leaps had a few people worried. The critics noticed the extent to which Baryshnikov had mastered—and was enjoying—the language of Balanchine. His performance so inspired Amy Carter that she decided to pick up her ballet slippers and take classes again. When President Carter asked the dancer how he managed to perform at the White House in the afternoon and then go straight to an evening performance at the Kennedy Center Misha replied, "You get some eggs and coffee and that's it."

Baryshnikov was pushing himself to the limit for Balanchine and for himself. He could see how movements that strained his capacity were easy for the other dancers, so he tried harder and harder to prove himself, despite the fact that his body hurt. Balanchine was no less relentless. He wanted Baryshnikov to do everything, to learn more and more new roles. He had always seen the process of learning to dance as a test not only of strength but also of commitment. Misha was committed and he was strong, but he no longer had the flexible muscles of a young dancer and he began to suffer from the tendonitis so common at the City Ballet.

As usual, ballet world gossip flourished. People said that Baryshnikov's flirtation with Balanchine's ballets was a failed experiment, and they attached much of the blame on Balanchine. The seventy-five-year-old ballet master had a reputation, fueled by rumor, for subtle cruelty and twisted relationships. He had alienated several dancers in his lifetime, he had messed up his five marriages, he had showered attention and affection on ballerinas and then suddenly and icily withdrawn his favors when he felt undermined, and now, people thought, he was making a point of humbling Baryshnikov. Misha insisted that this was not the case. Balanchine was always wonderful to him. Balanchine often invited Baryshnikov to his small apartment, where he lived a relatively Spartan life, and over dinners and glasses of vodka and schnapps they continued the relationship that had taken root at Saratoga Springs. Baryshnikov said later that his only regret was that he had not gone to Balanchine two years earlier.

Baryshnikov had another problem, a problem that in one way or another he had been dealing with since his dancing career began. He had never found an ideal partner. Nobody knows quite what it is that creates the dynamics of a great partnership. But always, behind the lifts and the catches and the ritual of flowers and kisses at curtain time, there either is or isn't magic. It can be the tension of two contrasting sensibilities or the perfect fit of likenesses. Misha couldn't soar with his partner if there was no eye contact, and there had to be just a hint of excitement, the possibility of more. When he danced with Gelsey Kirkland something flowed between them. The spark was there, but so was the danger that the spark might ignite. Some great male dancers are natural partners because of their courtesy and sensitivity to the ballerina. Baryshnikov was not that kind of partner; perhaps that was what Kirkland meant when she talked about there having been "two different egos in the room."

Misha's partnership with Patricia McBride was professional and sound, but it lacked excitement. Like Misha, she was a superb technician in her dancing, and she was one of the few ballerinas at the City Ballet short enough to dance with him. They had great respect for each other and they helped each other, but something was missing. Everyone could see that.

To open the spring season Misha danced in a restaging of Balanchine's *Apollo*, a role in which Peter Martins had reigned for ten years and one of the few roles in which Balanchine had predicted that Baryshnikov could excel. *Apollo* originated with Diaghilev in 1928, and it has always been seen as one of Balanchine's most crucial works. It is a sparse ballet, poetic and ritualistic. For the new season Balanchine had once again pruned the ballet, cutting it down to its barest essentials. Some Balanchine fans were outraged that he had tampered with the classic, and as a result there was as much attention paid to that scandal as there was to Baryshnikov's performance. Nevertheless, there was some exultation over Misha, who seemed to be almost wild with enjoyment in his role. "He gives us the sense that he is learning his own nature through the course of the dance," wrote Deborah Jowitt in the *Village Voice* on May 21, 1979.

By June 1979 Baryshnikov had learned and danced in twenty-two new ballets by Balanchine and Robbins. He had danced some of the greatest roles in the City Ballet repertoire and many in which critics felt he had been miscast. These were the *demi-caractère* roles, the kind of roles he had been given in his early Kirov years because of his build. The response to Baryshnikov's performances was still mixed. Friends in the company, like Peter Martins, insisted that Misha needed more time to make the transition, that his muscles would adapt and the pain in his knees and back would stop. Misha had been with the City Ballet for a year, and by now Balanchine was so ill that he could not walk.

Misha had a decision to make. Herman Krawitz, executive director of ABT, was looking for a new artistic director. Lucia Chase, at the age of seventy-three and after thirty-five years as "mother" and co-founder of the company, was stepping down under intense pressure from the board of directors. Since the company was in deep trouble after years of financial mismanagement, the new director would have to be something of a savior. Baryshnikov was on the list. So were a lot of other names, including that of Peter Martins, but Krawitz was behind Baryshnikov. They had produced *The Nutcracker* together, and the experience had convinced him that Baryshnikov had a talent for management. Besides, even his name would work wonders for ABT. Krawitz was convinced that Misha's star power would attract both donations and a large audience of fans.

Misha had been mulling it over. Sometimes he could make a

decision overnight, but this was different. To become the artistic
director of a company meant leaving the ranks, even if he continued to dance. It meant growing up suddenly, settling down,
and committing himself to a long-term responsibility. When he
thought about it, he had ideas for the company, things he would
like to do. But did he want to be in the position of an admin-
istrator? Did he want to trade in his jeans and T-shirts and cowboy boots for a suit and tie? Did he want to be the one who
everybody loves to hate? And did he want to leave the City
Ballet? Was he ready to give up?

Some people were speculating that Balanchine was planning
to install Baryshnikov as his successor at the City Ballet, although Baryshnikov did not really believe this. Nevertheless,
though Balanchine was ill, Baryshnikov decided to ask the master's opinion first. Balanchine's advice was simple: "You know,
dear, I think you should go." They both knew that the City
Ballet was not working out for him; Balanchine had probably
known it all along. On the other hand, ABT needed a lot of
cleaning up, and Baryshnikov had ideas. If they would let him
carry out those ideas, if he could make dancers dance his way
and people respect his mistakes, then that, said Balanchine, was
what he should do. Balanchine also told Baryshnikov that if
things didn't work out at ABT he could always come back, "because this is also your home." A couple of weeks later Balanchine
was admitted into the hospital for bypass surgery.

Baryshnikov still wasn't sure. He asked Peter Martins for his
advice. Martins told Baryshnikov that he should stay, that he
hadn't given himself time to develop under Balanchine. Martins
suggested that he remain with the company for another year or
two before taking ABT up on its offer.

On June 5 the press announced that ABT was considering Baryshnikov as Chase's successor. "Reliable sources" were quoted as
saying that Misha planned to remain with the City Ballet for the
season and one more year, and then take over the directorship
of ABT in September 1980. He had reportedly submitted condi-

tions for his acceptance and was rumored to be planning to retire from dance at the age of thirty-five.

Arrangements were finalized when Misha met Ballet Theatre's chairman of the board, Donald Kendall. Kendall was also chairman of the board at Pepsico, and during negotiations to build a Pepsico plant in the Soviet Union he had learned a great deal about Baryshnikov's native country, besides becoming a connoisseur of vodka. Baryshnikov and Kendall talked over dinner. Knowing his way to a Russian's heart, Kendall served smoked salmon from Iceland, vodka flavored with peppers from his own garden, and brandy that he had brought back from Russia—a brandy that Baryshnikov hadn't tasted in five years. "By three o'clock in the morning, everything was settled," recalls Kendall.

Once more the ballet world was thrown into confusion. While Misha finished the season with the City Ballet, summered with the company in Saratoga Springs, and toured with them to London in September, speculation erupted concerning the prospect of Baryshnikov—a thirty-two-year-old Russian superstar Casanova—directing the largest, most diverse, and most visible ballet company in America.

In October, after a Washington performance, the New York City Ballet announced that Baryshnikov would be leaving the company immediately instead of finishing out the year. Misha just couldn't take it any more. He felt that if he were to struggle any longer in the company he would lose his ability to do what he now knew he was best at—classical ballet. His tendonitis had grown much worse and he was suffering from injuries. In his estimation this experiment had already cost him a few years of his life as a dancer. "You think you could do anything," he said several years later, "and you can't. There are always limits, even for very gifted people. It's very hard to accept, but there's always an invisible ceiling above you and you should be careful not to go above it. You should jump into the water, but not without knowing how strong the current is." Now there was a new challenge ahead, and Misha had itchy feet again.

FIFTEEN

A Serious Man

WHEN *THE TURNING POINT* came out in 1977 Misha's Yuri represented the hope of the young generation in dance. Just two years later, during the two months that he spent considering the pros and cons of ABT's offer, Misha had begun to see himself as a dancer whose time was soon to come.

Physically Baryshnikov was almost past his prime, just at that time in his life where his character, his ability to communicate something to his audience besides the thrill of a virtuoso technique, had reached maturity. Inevitably, the theme of age and change—the only well-developed theme in the movie that had made him a Hollywood star—played an important role in Misha's decision to accept the ABT offer. He had decided to stop dancing soon, while he was still at his peak. He didn't want to finish his career as a has-been; dancing had never been such a compulsion for him that he couldn't stop when the time came. He was no fool. Yet, what would life be without dance? Misha could no longer afford to ignore that nagging question. He needed something other than his own stage career to care about, some kind of responsibility beyond that which he had always felt toward himself as a dancer. He needed to be needed. In a sense, it was a matter of growing up.

Misha felt more settled now than he had felt since pulling up his Russian roots in 1974. During his fifteen months with the City Ballet he had toured much less than in previous years with ABT, and New York had begun to feel like home. His nostalgia for the old life had faded. During a visit to Tokyo in the summer he had seen the Kirov, both in performance and walking in tight groups through the streets; he watched them from his car window, but he didn't stop to talk. His trip to China, where he performed, taught a master class, and saw only misery and scarcity, was a real "anti-nostalgia pill."

His relationship with Jessica Lange, while still open, had settled down, too. Their life wasn't the jet-set life of Baryshnikov's first years in the West. It was more subdued, more relaxed. They made efforts to protect their privacy; they escaped to the country whenever they could and at parties they tended to sink into the furniture. When Lange went to Oregon to film *How to Beat the High Cost of Living* in the fall of 1979 they exchanged long, loving phone calls. In fact, it was during one such phone conversation that director Bob Rafelson knocked on Lange's motel room door. He had come miles in his search for a Cora to star opposite Jack Nicholson in his remake of *The Postman Always Rings Twice*. He was looking for an actress to match Lana Turner's steamy Cora, someone who could spark Nicholson's own sullen sexuality.

Rafelson sat in Lange's tiny, seedy motel room, waiting and watching. Sprawled casually across the bed, almost oblivious of this big Hollywood director, Lange was talking long distance to Baryshnikov. She talked for almost an hour. By the time she finally put down the phone and turned her attention to him, Rafelson was convinced that Lange, with her powerful, effortless sensuality, was the actress he'd been looking for. In

November, just as Baryshnikov left the City Ballet, Lange went to Santa Barbara to film *Postman*.

After more than five years in the West Misha had made friends—that is, friends as he defined them. These were people he could talk to, whatever his mood, people who made him welcome in their kitchens if, on the way home from work or on some lonely evening when Jessica was out of town, he felt like dropping by and chatting about his day. Several old friends from Russia were now in America—Nina Alovert, the theatrical photographer in whose Leningrad kitchen he had regularly sat eating homemade dumplings and musing on life and love and Tanya Koltsova; Elena Tchernichova, who had separated from her husband, Igor; and even Misha's old teacher from Riga, Bella Kovarskaya, who had found her way to America and went to see Baryshnikov in New York. Kovarskaya brought with her a part of Misha's childhood; here was someone who had known him when he was twelve years old, and she had not only recollections but also pictures of Misha as a child with all of his old classmates. "He was so excited to see those pictures," recalls Kovarskaya. "He was dancing around like a boy, he was so happy."

In August 1979 Alexander Godunov—Baryshnikov's boyhood classmate in Riga—defected in New York during a Bolshoi tour and soon after that joined ABT under Baryshnikov's directorship. His defection rivaled Baryshnikov's for dramatic content in that it centered on the decision of his wife and fellow dancer, Ludmila, to return to the Soviet Union. For three days U.S. officials at New York's Kennedy Airport detained the Soviet airline Aeroflot jet with Ludmila plus fifty-two other passengers on board, trying to gain her assurance that she was not being forced to return home. The diplomatic tug-of-war nearly touched off an international incident, and created a blaze of publicity that helped launch the flamboyant Godunov's American career. Baryshnikov and Godunov were never close friends. In fact, there was from the beginning a hint of rivalry in their relationship which would later become the subject of ballet gossip. Nevertheless Godunov, like Kovarskaya, represented a piece of Misha's past. His presence at ABT may have helped Misha to restore a sense of rootedness.

Rudolf Nureyev had become a friend. Although they had never met in Russia, the two superstars shared many memories— the Vaganova school and the Kirov stage, the narrow bed in Pushkin's apartment, the trauma of defection. Baryshnikov frequently stayed at Nureyev's London home, and although the relationship cooled at times—"He's not an easy man," Misha said about his attention-grabbing compatriot—Baryshnikov admitted that many of the risks he had taken in life, from leaving Russia to breaking away from classical ballet and making his first Hollywood movie, were inspired by Nureyev's example.

Misha's home was now in America. He had a car and an American driver's license, and he had two dogs to walk every morning in Central Park—La Goulue, who was by now a mother of ten, and Katia, a golden retriever. The dogs were his family, the constants in his life. They rooted him. They appeared with Misha in photographs and sometimes in the studio. When Misha turned up at Natalia Makarova's birthday party, La Goulue was his partner. Misha had modernized his Park Avenue apartment and had bought a country house in northwestern Connecticut, a kind of Americanized dacha which he loved dearly. He spent as much time there as he was able, often spending two or three days at a time chasing his dogs through the woods and reading books from his growing library in front of the fireplace. His English had improved immensely. He was past the point of slang and TV talk; it was his language now, metaphors and all. "You want to do the same ravioli, but better quality," he said of his plans for ABT.

Beyond the occasional metaphor Baryshnikov didn't publicize his plans for ABT. Nobody knew quite what to expect, yet almost everyone had a theory. The rumors began immediately. It has been said that late spring is "silly season" in New York's ballet world, and with silly season comes inevitable gossip. In the spring of 1979 the gossip was clearly focused on Misha's plans to return to ABT, just as in the previous spring it had focused on Baryshnikov and Balanchine. Why was he leaving the City Ballet? Didn't he and Patty McBride get along? Or had his ego been hurt by Balanchine? Had he been missing Gelsey? And would Gelsey, who had canceled many of her ABT engagements and in May gone on an "unofficial sick leave," pull herself together and return to ABT to partner Misha?

As silly season passed, anxieties and speculation overtook the gossip. What kind of director would Baryshnikov make? Suddenly Misha's image as America's most desirable ballet idol, the Russian heartbreaker, was seriously backfiring. While he was highly respected as the greatest dancer in the world and was popular for his funny clowning and his one-of-the-guys manner, people both inside and outside the company found it hard to take seriously the idea of Baryshnikov as an important artistic director. They couldn't help but still see him as the young twenty-six-year-old who chased girls and money, because that was the image he had continued to project.

Even those who knew him better wondered. Would he be able to combine stardom with administration? As a thirty-two-year-old dancer did he have enough experience to do the job well? Could he be trusted to take care of the company before his own career, or would he transform ABT into his own training ground? In fact, would he be around at all, or would he continue to indulge himself with twenty-five-thousand-dollar guest appearances and television specials? It was certainly a huge responsibility. Baryshnikov was to be entrusted with the careers of ninety dancers, a complex seventeen-week touring schedule, a repertoire of seventy-five ballets, a budget of over $10 million, and a highly visible American company—America's primary ballet export—with a distinguished forty-year history.

Baryshnikov's very Russianness was seen as a potential problem. Did he understand American dance well enough to preserve and nurture the company's avowed American spirit, or would he turn it into a copy of the Kirov? "The American Ballet Theatre as we have known it for 40 years will cease to exist," warned Lucia Chase's co-director, Oliver Smith. He forecast that Baryshnikov would neglect the American ballets in ABT's repertoire in order to concentrate on the old Russian classics, those "great old dinosaurs" with which he had grown up. Others worried that Baryshnikov would be unduly influenced by his Russian émigré friends, that he wouldn't be loyal to Ballet Theatre's American tradition.

Perhaps there was a basic feeling that Baryshnikov couldn't commit himself to anything for long enough to make it work. He hated waiting. Misha had left the Kirov, he'd left his country, he'd left ABT, he'd left the City Ballet, and he'd left numerous women. He had a short attention span. He sucked up new experiences like a vacuum cleaner, but once the novelty wore off, he lost interest. His mind was always searching for new excitement. Maybe this made him the kind of dancer he was, but the role of artistic director demanded a certain stability and perseverance.

While the ballet world reflected, Misha took a two-week Caribbean vacation, then returned to New York and set to work. He had another project to prepare, and for Misha, the preparations were always the most exciting part of any project. He was taking singing classes and tap-dancing classes, practicing up to six hours a day; he was learning to be Baryshnikov on Broadway. Herman Krawitz, in the role of executive producer, had come up with a scheme for a money-making television special starring Baryshnikov as his winsome Russian self, gazing nostalgically through the looking glass of a dance rehearsal studio into the glorious past of the Broadway musical. As his guide through the looking glass Baryshnikov chose his friend Liza Minnelli (firmly denied rumors of a romance between the two had proliferated two years earlier, shortly before Minelli's marriage to producer Mark Gero).

"Baryshnikov on Broadway," sponsored by IBM and televised

by ABC on April 24, 1980, was Misha's tribute to the genius of
the American musical comedy, a form that has fascinated him
ever since his first taste of Hollywood musicals as a boy in Riga:
"I loved the combination of theater and dancing, the lights, the
sets, the money—it was a capitalist paradise." His heroes are
performers like James Cagney and Fred Astaire, the tough guys
who danced like angels. "When I first saw Mr. Astaire's movies,
it was very discouraging," he recalls. "I thought everybody in
America was that good. I felt, 'You're never gonna dance, kid.'"
And he has immense admiration for the talents of the Broadway
gypsies who can sing, dance, and tap dance all at the same time.

"Baryshnikov on Broadway" was Misha's fantasy realized. He
could finally be a Boadway dancer, an archetypal American. As
he said in the production, "You know, I've been a Puppet in
Petroushka, a Slave in La Corsaire, a Prince in the Nutcracker—
but one thing I've never been is a full-fledged American cowboy
with hats, boots, and everything." In the fifty-four-minute show
choreographed by Ron Feld, Misha whirled through a medley of
Broadway classics from *Oklahoma!* to *Guys and Dolls.* Like his heroes, he danced, acted, and sang—in voice that sounded more
like Marlene Dietrich than Frank Sinatra. He even had the opportunity to dance with the cast of *A Chorus Line,* as just another
Broadway gypsy. In her June 1980 review for *Dancemagazine*
Norma McLain Stoop wrote, "It's as a line dancer in 'One Sin-
gular Sensation' that he's most impressive. . . . Baryshnikov becomes that one gypsy you nudge your friend about—the kid
you know positively will make it one day."

Misha liked to see himself as the kid from nowhere who gets
to sit at the stars' table through sheer raw talent. He made
friends with eighty-year-old James Cagney, his tough-guy hero.
As a kid in Riga he had stood in the ticket line for eight hours to
see a Cagney movie. Now they were spending Thanksgiving together at Baryshnikov's Connecticut home—they were buddies.
In 1979, when Baryshnikov sheepishly showed him a rough cut

of his show, Cagney's comment was, "Not bad!" In 1986 Baryshnikov would be one of the four pall-bearers at Cagney's funeral.

There were some, however, including a few of Misha's friends, who felt that "Baryshnikov on Broadway" represented a trivialization of the great dancer's talents, a symptom of his almost indiscriminate infatuation with the cultural products of the American dream, the capitalist paradise. What became known as the Americanization of Baryshnikov was seen as the cheapening of his image. He could not reproduce the purely American genius of Broadway. But he had to try. Misha was infatuated by his fantasy of Broadway and its gypsies. Broadway was popular culture and its stars and chorus lines were just regular guys, whereas the classical dancer, says Misha, is always a loner, always self-involved.

Almost a year passed between Misha's sudden departure from the City Ballet in the fall of 1979 and his assumption of the ABT directorship in the fall of 1980. It was a period notable for Baryshnikov's absence from the world of ballet. During the late spring ABT celebrated its fortieth anniversary with a ten-week season at the Metropolitan Opera House, including a dazzling dance gala night. From all over the world Ballet Theatre stars past and present came to pay their respects. The press noted that Baryshnikov was "conspicuously absent." The only sign of him was a congratulatory telegram. Was Misha displaying great courtesy in allowing Lucia Chase to reign supreme over the proceedings, people wondered? Or was he simply too busy with his guest appearances and movies and musicals and television projects?

In fact, except for his television special in April, one unscheduled appearance in May with the City Ballet and a disappointing guest appearance as Romeo with London's Royal Ballet (according to critic Arlene Croce, Baryshnikov was glib, plump, and complacent), Misha *was* conspicuously absent from the stage during his year between companies. He hardly danced at all.

Misha was recovering his energy. He was worn down from the struggle of the City Ballet and from all of the criticism of the past two years. He wasn't used to it. Besides, he needed to prepare himself for his new role in life as a man of responsibility. His image was a major consideration; he had to make people take him seriously. When the time came to look through publicity shots of himself with photographer Martha Swope, he avoided pictures in which he was smiling. "I'm a serious man now!" he reportedly said. Misha was planning what was later described as a "revolution" in the form of a five-year plan on the scale of Mikhail Gorbachev's *Perestroika*. Balanchine had told him that ABT needed a clean-up, and Baryshnikov was about to start sweeping the floors.

The first phase of his plan was aimed at undoing the star system of which he himself had been a part. Star dancers at ABT did the company no good in the long run, he felt. Many had taken unfair advantage of their positions, demanding roles for which they were not suited and partners who had to be imported, and then disappearing at the first opportunity of high-paying guest appearances. They had no self-discipline or sense of proportion, Misha reasoned. And while the stars grabbed all of the best roles and all of the attention, the younger dancers in the corps, who needed direction more than the stars, were left on their own. Like the chorus line, the corps de ballet is an integral part of the show, and it has to be cohesive. There was a visible difference between a Kirov or City Ballet performance, where the entire ensemble danced with precision and unity of purpose, and an ABT performance, where the stars stood out while the corps struggled along in the background.

Misha had in mind a company run more along the lines of the City Ballet, where the individual, no matter how talented, defers to the good of the whole. His vision, like Balanchine's, was fundamentally influenced by his Kirov background. Perhaps this is what gave him the single-mindedness to be almost ruthless in carrying out his plan. The Kirov was great; it produced the greatest dancers in the world. He knew that his own success was due in part to the extraordinarily high level of discipline imposed by the Soviet system. He would bring that kind of discipline to ABT. He wanted to turn Ballet Theatre into the greatest company in the world, and he knew that was going to be tough.

From the very beginning Misha approached his job like a mission, reluctantly yet keenly. He envisaged a beautiful corps de ballet, a perfect line of tall, leggy ballerinas dancing in total harmony. The height was needed, he said, because ABT danced on large stages and because he intended to concentrate initially on the grand nineteenth-century story ballets, such as *Swan Lake*. "I would like to see these ballets more glamorous, more classy," he said, and that meant weeding out the corps members who may have worked on their technique for years but were not blessed with his preferred body type. Misha received some stinging criticism for his firing of several dancers in the corps. Like Balanchine, whose concept of glamor he seemed to be emulating, Baryshnikov was accused of propogating a tendency in American ballet that leads to dietary deficiencies amongst young dancers who feel compelled to practically starve themselves in order to fit a director's aesthetic. But this was Baryshnikov's prerogative; it was up to him, as the new director, to shape the company as he felt fit.

From the moment ABT members discovered that some dancers' contracts had not been renewed, there was panic. Other dancers decided not to continue at ABT under the Baryshnikov regime. He insisted that principals, who had previously been paid on a lucrative per-performance basis, must now sign seasonal contracts. He warned that dancers who acted irresponsibly would be fired. He didn't feel good about this, but he gritted his teeth, determined to be tough.

In July Baryshnikov announced his administrative appointments. One of those, promoting Charles France—previously the press officer and Misha's spokesman—to the position of assistant to the artistic director, caused still more dismay. France was seen

by many ABT dancers as an intelligent but overbearing and su-
percritical balletomane, a dictator stalking the corridors and or-
dering last-minute changes in makeup and costumes. Dancers
were anxious that as second in command France would virtually
control the company—especially if Baryshnikov wasn't around.
They were also worried about his influence on the new director.
France and Baryshnikov had been buddies since 1974; they'd
spent all of their time together on tours, often over a bottle of
vodka. Everyone knew that Baryshnikov always listened to
France.

Then Natalia Makarova, who had returned to ABT as a star
dancer, announced that she was going to establish her own company, possibly taking with her some of the major principal dancers from ABT. The stars were unhappy. They felt betrayed by
Baryshnikov and didn't want to work for him. Makarova's troupe
eventually collapsed, but for the time being, confusion took
over. This was a defection of huge proportions, and it reflected
badly on Baryshnikov.

Misha found himself in an awkward position. Many of the
dancers whose fate now lay in his hands had been and still were
his friends. While he emphasized that his attitude toward his
friends as people had not changed, a couple of years later he had
to admit that "a new situation may have changed their point of
view about the relationship." There was something dispassionate
in the way Misha claimed to separate business from pleasure and
friends as people from friends as professional dancers. Yet when
it came right down to it, when he wanted to take a cherished
role from a principal or fire an older soloist, he was evasive. He
just could not bring himself to break the news; sometimes France
had to do the job instead. When the personal confrontations
became really tough, Krawitz would be called in to help.

One spring evening Baryshnikov had dinner with Gelsey
Kirkland, whom he hadn't seen in months. He invited her to
rejoin ABT, but according to Kirkland he didn't say how he intended to use her in the company, either over dinner or later,

when he invited her to spend an evening at his country home. Kirkland assumed that they would pick up their partnership where they had left off, but gradually she came to realize that Baryshnikov was avoiding the issue. He couldn't tell her that although they would dance together once in a while, they would no longer be a partnership. He had scheduled Kirkland to partner Patrick Bissell during the first ABT performances of the season in Washington.

During the summer, in the midst of the confusion surrounding Baryshnikov's new job, Jessica Lange discovered that she was pregnant. The news came as something of a shock; neither she nor Baryshnikov had intended to have a baby, and they didn't know how long their relationship would last. Baryshnikov was immersed in Ballet Theatre and would soon be touring again; Lange's career was on the rise. Both understood the strain of being separated for weeks and even months. Yet there was no question about continuing the pregnancy. Lange was ecstatic. There had been a void in her life, and she hoped a baby might fill it. She was thirty-one years old and now was the best time to have a baby. As for Baryshnikov, he was thirty-two and had never been responsible for anyone but himself. He had grown up without a family and without the human tension of family commitments. In a way he hadn't grown up at all—he still felt like a kid. Now, just as the full dimensions of his Ballet Theatre job were dawning, Misha was going to become a father. It began to seem as if this was one of the most important things that had ever happened to him.

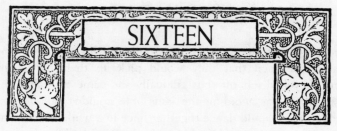

SIXTEEN

White Nights,
Black Nights

MISHA WAS GOING to be a father, but not to his ballet company. Lucia Chase had treated the dancers as a family over which she presided as a kind of matriarch, but Misha wanted to see his company as a group of professional adults working as a team. Instead of a sprawling, hierarchical household, Ballet Theatre was to become an institution. Misha instituted a system of individual worksheets to keep track of how hard everyone was working and warning letters to inform dancers of imminent dismissal. Computers were programmed to take over the complex job of scheduling rehearsals. He made it clear that he expected every dancer to take company class every day, no matter how tired they were or how badly their muscles ached. Like a strict new principal in a school full of unruly kids, Baryshnikov made quite an impression.

As the first rehearsal period began, everything was in disarray. The building housing the company's studios had been demolished during the summer layoff, and Ballet Theatre's new downtown studios, on Nineteenth and Broadway, were still under construction. For the first few weeks of the season ABT worked in the studios at Radio City Music Hall. The dancers thought it was pretty funny; they were using the same stage door as the Rockettes. As soon as he could, Baryshnikov moved the company down to Nineteenth Street, and work started in earnest.

A lot of people were surprised by Baryshnikov's very definite presence around the new studios. He took company class every morning and sometimes taught the class, he attended and danced in rehearsals, he coached, he wandered in and out of studios checking on a pas de deux here and a new solo there. Chase had always left those jobs up to the choreographers and teachers, preferring to conduct affairs from her office. Baryshnikov, on the other hand, spent as little time as possible in his office. He hated to sit still, particularly when there were was so much to be done, and so quickly.

Baryshnikov soon became known as the "great noncommunicator"—just as the "great communicator," Ronald Reagan, was moving into the White House. He had no time for chat or for comforting words, and he seldom tried to explain himself to the company. Very few of the dancers realized how uncomfortable he felt in his new role; instead, they saw him as aloof. His corrections were terse, occasionally stony, consisting of just a couple of words. His response to foolishness and laziness could be scathing. Irresponsibility upset him so much that sometimes he would fly into a rage. He would set the most exacting standards, and he was impatient. At times, and to some dancers, he seemed unapproachable; many of them eventually left. On the other hand, there were those who were not bothered by Baryshnikov's manner. Asked about the director's communication problem one dancer answered, "It depends on how hard you listen."

When the work was going well, when the energy level was high and everyone was willing to aim for perfection, Baryshnikov was one of them. And the fact that he was there with them as a dancer, sweating as much as they were in class, in rehearsal, and on stage, made it all worthwhile. They looked up to him as the greatest dancer in the world. It was a thrill to be taught by him, to dance near him, even to be corrected by him—and then again, it could be a crushing experience. His mood could swing suddenly, at the slightest annoyance.

Baryshnikov had canceled the regular fall season in New York in order to give the company several extra weeks of hard work before they went public. It was the longest rehearsal period in ABT history. He had decided to start out by overhauling the Russian classics—those old dinosaurs—that were his territory and his roots. He felt perfectly secure in them, completely invincible. He knew exactly what had to be done. He wanted to teach what he had learned at the Kirov—that dancing the classics is a theatrical art involving not just movement but also the expression of emotion. He left copies of the ballet stories outside studio doors, with instructions that they were to be read. He took pains to explain the nuances of each role. When words failed he used mime and impersonation to demonstrate the subtle shifts in character or feeling he was looking for. He could do all of the characters from *Don Quixote*. "It was fascinating to watch him switch back and forth," Robert LaFosse remembers in his autobiography *Nothing to Hide*, "and then to see the dancers do their imitations of what he had done. He was a one-man gallery of character studies."

And all the time Baryshnikov was watching, looking to see who would make it and who would not. He had to admit that it was all a hunch—a sense of musicality here, an unusual face there. Just as often it was a question of attitude; he was interested in dancers who were committed, professional, and self-disciplined. He was looking for the new generation.

His policy from the beginning was to promote young, often teenage dancers from the lower rungs of the company hierarchy rather than to import ready-made stars. He called them "kids"; many of them were fresh out of ballet school, so they were appreciative of his attention and the opportunities he gave them. Unlike the stars, these dancers were undemanding. They knew that at any time Baryshnikov might summon them from the corps dressing room and try them out in a solo or principal role. If they did well they were eventually promoted to principal status. Until then they returned to the corps corridors, where they faced the inevitable jealousies of the other members. Meanwhile, the more established principal dancers were saying that their own careers were being neglected while the kids were being pushed into an early limelight that would stunt their growth as mature artists.

Baryshnikov introduced the new generation suddenly, on the first night of ABT's seventeen-week winter tour, the first performance under his directorship. The company was due to open on December 10 at the Kennedy Center with Gelsey Kirkland and Patrick Bissell, who had become drug-dependent lovers in preceding months. The two were scheduled for a full dress rehearsal in the afternoon of the ninth. They finally arrived that night, high on cocaine.

Kirkland and Bissell had been given several warnings about punctuality, and this time, on the eve of the opening everyone had been waiting for, Baryshnikov gave orders for them to be dismissed at once. It was a shock for the entire company. America's star ballerina was fired by Herman Krawitz and the company manager in a Watergate Hotel room. The firing was professional and cold, and Baryshnikov was not present. The ABT star system was now dead.

Kirkland claims that during the several times he coached her in the studio Baryshnikov must have recognized the signs of her drug problem—shaking legs, runny nose, wads of tissues lying around the studio—but he chose not to acknowledge it. Even after she had been rehired and fired again twice, nobody at ABT addressed her problem, except that Baryshnikov obliquely suggested that she separate work and play. According to Ballet Theatre, Baryshnikov's policy was aimed at preserving the dancer's right to privacy. His only concern was how the dancers performed professionally; their personal lives had nothing to do with him. On the other hand, Kirkland was a friend. Was Baryshnikov afraid of a drug scandal, as Kirkland has suggested, or was he evading personal involvement in what he saw as Gelsey's problem? As one critic said, "The question was not whether she could make it to the top, but whether she would self-destruct first." Cocaine was merely one symptom of a problem that Baryshnikov had already walked out on.

When ABT opened on December 10, in place of Kirkland the audience at Kennedy Center saw Susan Jaffe, an eighteen-year-old corps member with a dark, alluring beauty, partnering Alexander Godunov. They also saw the debut of Robert LaFosse, in a role that on other nights would be Baryshnikov's—Balanchine's *Prodigal Son*. The critics were amazed at the sudden appearance of these two extremely talented young dancers, but they also were skeptical. They knew that it could take years for even a technically brilliant dancer to develop a mature presence on stage. Was Baryshnikov preparing LaFosse, with his young, blond Grecian god looks, to take his place as a performer? La Fosse was subsequently cast in several trademark Baryshnikov roles, and he excelled. But some feel that it was all too much too fast for the twenty-one-year-old, and in 1985 he left ABT on the verge of a nervous breakdown.

After LaFosse, Baryshnikov began to develop a new protégé, Gil Boggs. But this time he had more experience. He was still promoting young dancers, but more gently. Misha was dancing less and learning to deal more even-handedly with the morning to night headaches of running a company—the hirings and firings, the contract negotiations, the dental plans, the production meetings, the terrible sessions with a contentious board of directors, the complaints and injuries of his dancers. As he grew more secure he became more generous in his manner. He had come under criticism from inside and outside the company, he had made enemies, and he had had to face the outcomes of some of his judgments. "It makes you grow up very fast," he admitted in the fall of 1987.

By this time Misha was the adoring father of a little girl.

On March 5, 1981, Jessica Lange walked twenty blocks through a gentle March snowstorm to tell her doctor that she was having contractions. Then, when he told her it was nothing, she walked the twenty blocks back home. Two hours later she gave birth to an eight-pound daughter. It happened so fast that she didn't even have time to call Baryshnikov, who was touring with his company in Buffalo, New York. When she reached him he flew back to New York immediately, thrilled. The couple named the baby Alexandra (Misha sometimes spells it Aleksandra), a good Russian name: his mother's name. Since Alexandra was such a mouthful for a small baby, they began to call her by the Russian diminutive Shura.

During the summer Lange and Baryshnikov looked for another country house, a family home. They settled on a turn-of-the-century converted barn surrounded by five acres of hilly land strewn with wild flowers and ferns, on a bluff overlooking the Hudson River. Sneden's Landing is a perfect hideaway for semireclusive stars (Ellen Burstyn and Al Pacino were inconspicuous neighbors). Wide driveways lead off the highway at decent intervals and disappear into the trees. Driving fast in his silver-gray Mercedes convertible, Misha could reach the "red barn" from Manhattan in just twenty-five minutes, and yet it was secluded and idyllic—a relatively simple house with three bedrooms, three bathrooms, huge windows, and a wisteria arbor over the driveway. Misha still had his Park Avenue apartment, full of beautiful antiques and books, but he rarely slept there. He didn't like to be alone. He preferred to drive full speed away from the tension of the city to the home that was always somewhere in the back of his mind.

Shura was very much her mother's baby. In a series of interviews Lange described her daughter as the most important thing in her life, the person with whom she most wanted to be, her ultimate joy. In the winter, when Shura was less than a year old, Baryshnikov went on tour again while Lange and the baby went to Los Angeles where she had rented a home for a few months. She hated Los Angeles, but this time it didn't matter. She had been offered the role of Frances Farmer, the role she'd wanted so much and always knew she would get some day. She'd spent her New York years researching the rebellious actress's frenzied life and death, so it didn't really surprise her when she won the role over Meryl Streep, Jane Fonda, Sissy Spacek, and Diane Keaton. Frances was her personal obsession—she felt there was some sort of "cosmic connection" there. The movie was to be directed by Graeme Clifford—as *Postman*'s film editor he admitted to having fallen "a bit in love" with Lange—and Sam Shepard was to play Harry York. Lange packed her bags, her dog, her canary, and her baby and set off for Hollywood. It was going to be a long, intense winter.

Misha's second year as artistic director was beginning, under the close scrutiny of the ballet world. He had made many behind-the-scenes changes: turned the company from a fractious family into a large, homogenized institution; arranged open auditions and restricted the number of students at the ABT school so that he could offer full scholarships to all; brought in special coaches, many of them Russian, and introduced the teaching of character dance; with the help of his coaches, begun to teach Soviet-style classes based on Vaganova's rigorous system; and tried to implement a policy of equality among dancers, in which a twenty-year-old corps member could share a role with a forty-year-old principal.

Most of these changes could be traced directly back to the Kirov and to Soviet dance in general. Lucia Chase's "family" had become Baryshnikov's "regime." It was as if Russia's national identity were at stake. Even the controversial policy of promoting from the corps was a Kirov policy implemented after Misha's departure. But the most controversial topic of Misha's first season centered around his restagings of some of the Russian story ballets.

The Russian classics in the ABT repertoire existed in versions that the West had inherited near the turn of the century via a man named Nicholai Sergeyev. Sergeyev was a *régisseur*, or ballet notator, at the Kirov. When he left Russia by train in 1912, following Diaghilev, he smuggled with him a number of the Kirov ballets in the form of a trunk full of notes. These he took to London's Royal Ballet, where he became its *régisseur*, and from there the ballets were passed down to ABT. By the time Baryshnikov learned the classics at the Kirov, they no longer resembled the original versions that Sergeyev had taken to London. They had evolved naturally through time in the hands of some of the Kirov dancers and ballet masters, including Misha's old director, Konstantin Sergeyev.

It was these contemporary Soviet versions that Misha restaged at ABT, adapting and streamlining them in the process. Whether they called the results "trivialized" and "show biz" or "Sovietized," critics were horrified. Baryshnikov had betrayed the purity of the ABT repertoire by replacing the originals with versions imported from Russia, and he had even tampered with the Soviet versions! Misha argued on both fronts; his tradition was being attacked. The Kirov versions, he said, were just as pure as those that Nicholai Sergeyev had exported. Besides, ballets must change with the times, and every generation should be free to add something original to a classic. He was not interested in curating a choreographic museum.

In Baryshnikov's view, ballet had the potential to grow into a hugely popular form of American entertainment, and to this end there was no harm in deleting boring acts or scenes from *Swan Lake* or *Sleeping Beauty*. His opinion was widely viewed as utterly cynical, yet it was a policy that Misha stubbornly insisted he would continue.

In the spring of 1982 Baryshnikov rehired Patrick Bissell and Gelsey Kirkland, despite the fact that they had become the joke of the ballet world, and restaged *Giselle*—minus the dramatically tedious act one Peasant Pas de Deux that, ironically, he had danced as his Kirov debut. But there was an even more signifi-

cant change: Misha had reinterpreted his famous Albrecht. Instead of the love-torn youth who had danced his heart out at the
Kirov and had later taken the New World by storm, now his
Albrecht was the aristocratic cynic playing with the love of
Kirkland's frail, cocaine-inspired Giselle. Questioned by a surprised critic Baryshnikov responded, "I just changed my mind."
He was different now, he said. He was older, cooler. Passion
did not come so naturally any more; what remained was a desire
for that most elusive of creatures, woman.

"I may quit dancing tomorrow," Baryshnikov said in the spring
of 1982, "I may go on." Dancing, he said, was just a job for him
now. Misha wanted to read more, see more. He wanted to be
with his daughter. His family, he said, was now his main joy in
life; it was something he'd missed ever since he was a boy. Yet
he'd been apart from them all winter. Perhaps, he said, he would
like to stop everything and disappear to the country with
Jessica, Alexandra, and his dogs. Perhaps he could be happy
playing, listening to music, fishing, reading. Shura was growing
up. She was picking up his accent, and Misha was learning how
to be a father.

"I think parenting came naturally to him," Lange said, adding
that of course she was the one who was really raising the baby,
that she was the one who spent time with her. After months of
legal battles Lange had won her divorce from Paco Grande.
Misha was talking about marriage, but Jessica was hesitant to
make another legal commitment. She didn't want to bring the
baby up by herself, but as she said, it depended on Misha. They
were apart so much. Alexandra was her main concern now, and
she wanted her daughter to have a close-to-normal country
childhood. She'd had a log cabin built near her parents' home in
Minnesota, a genuine retreat with no phone or television or
neighbors, and she was thinking of buying land in New Mexico.
"Maybe I'll retire to Taos and paint," she said. Filming *Frances* had
drained her. She was tired and confused about her life. There
had been so many changes.

Misha was now the oldest male dancer in the company, and he was not in great shape. He said that dancing with Balanchine had taught him a new way of moving and relating to music. He was no longer interested in acrobatics; although his dancing was still spectacular, he had cut many of the dazzling leaps and spins from his roles.

In February, Baryshnikov had torn the cartilege in his right knee, a painful and serious injury requiring microsurgery and regular physical therapy. He had been working too hard, pushing himself in too many directions, and going home to an empty house most of the winter. Misha was on the sidelines for almost two months. When he was able, he watched the kids rehearse and hesitantly tried to demonstrate steps. It was demoralizing. He put on weight. He was tired. He began to take time off. Misha was trying to develop an appetite for a normal life-style.

In the corridors and offices of Ballet Theatre a nagging doubt was being voiced: did Misha care any more? Things were shaky after a full year of drastic change, and while in his first year Misha's presence had held the pieces together, now his absence created a void that was filled with whispers of dissent. Misha had demanded total commitment, but where was he? When he was there, he remained remote and inaccessible to the dancers— many of them very young, overworked, and emotionally dependent on the company, their only world. They needed someone to whom they could turn, and they resented having to go to Charles France instead of dealing directly with Baryshnikov. If Baryshnikov tended to be short and sharp in his responses, France reportedly bordered on the brutal. One dancer described him as the company's own KGB. The three Russian assistants to whom Baryshnikov had delegated responsibility for coaching and company class were contradicting one another; sometimes they refused to even speak to one another.

In June 1982 Alexander Godunov heard through his agent, Keith Addis, that his ABT contract would not be renewed for the following season. The reason cited was that he was no longer needed in the company and that, as Godunov's press release stated, "in the opinion of Mr. Baryshnikov, artistic director of ABT, they do not have a good relationship." The news stunned a lot of people, including Godunov. He had just completed his third year with Ballet Theatre, and although in the beginning his dramatic defection story had made him something of a scene-stealer, he had become an integral part of the company. He was ready to learn new ballets, he said, but nothing new was being offered. Why was he being fired?

The most hurtful part of it was not why, but how. Baryshnikov had said nothing to Godunov about his intentions. According to Godunov, speaking to John Gruen for the September 1982 issue of *Dancemagazine*, "nobody had the guts to face me personally." Baryshnikov and Godunov had never been great friends, but neither had there been any serious conflict between them. Besides, they had known each other since childhood. Godunov was not alone in feeling that Baryshnikov owed him an explanation. It reminded him of the way people dealt with one another in the Soviet Union. "It was done as if I were a piece of furniture," he told Gruen. "Only a week before the announcement I went in to see Charles France, Misha's assistant, and he told me we'd be talking about next season in a matter of days. Then came the message about my services no longer being required."

After an indignant flurry in the ballet world ABT tried to patch things up; Godunov was merely being asked to take a leave of absence, Baryshnikov announced, and the two had always shared the "warmest feelings." Nevertheless, neither Baryshnikov nor anyone else from ABT management actually spoke directly to Godunov. As far as Godunov was concerned he had been put out into the cold. He never returned to Ballet Theatre. Gelsey Kirkland, still high on cocaine, also found herself without a contract.

It was all so impersonal, so unsettling. Punctuality, perfection, and self-discipline were continually stressed as the kind of professional behavior expected by management, but some of the young dancers complained that what they really needed was the inspiration that they had once found in their heroes and heroines, the ballet stars of Lucia Chase's company. And whereas Chase had been there for the dancers, ready with congratulations after every performance, now the dancers danced, went home to sleep, struggled to get back for class the next morning, got paid, and danced again. It was just a job.

In the fall of 1982 Baryshnikov ran into Gelsey Kirkland. Having "escaped" from a psychiatric institution, she had continued her spiral down the tunnel of cocaine abuse. She'd been performing as a guest artist around the country, stumbling on and off stages while the critics watched, aghast. Flirting with disaster in Harlem, she'd watched her body swell and crumble in response to the drugs. She'd even suffered brain seizures. "I miss you," Baryshnikov told her. "There's nobody to give me a hard time anymore!" In November he rehired her. She couldn't understand why. She was a washout, and she knew it.

In fact, everyone was giving Baryshnikov a hard time. The board of directors had begun to worry. Obvious connections were being made between Misha's policies as a director, particularly his no-star policy, and the fact that the company was in the red. The public missed the glamor of the old Ballet Theatre; during an ambitious eleven-week season in New York almost half of the seats remained empty. Morale was low throughout the company. The board could see that when Baryshnikov wasn't around, the dancing suffered. For a while it looked as if ABT might even fold.

Misha was in the process of staging the most expensive ballet in ABT history, *Cinderella*, for the 1983 winter season. Conceived and choreographed by Baryshnikov in collaboration with free-lance choreographer Peter Anastos, it was to be a lavish spectacle. A quarter of a million dollars was spent on costumes, one hundred thousand dollars of that on wigs alone; the whole production cost close to a million dollars. *Cinderella* was going to save the day. The question now was whether the artistic director would still be around.

Alexandra had been tagging along with her mother while she filmed *Tootsie* in New York, and with her father to theaters and rehearsal halls. "She *explodes* when she sees the dancing," said Lange. But while Lange was thinking more and more about raising a family and about "generations caring for generations," Alexandra's father was more and more submerged in the difficulties of his dual role as ballet star and artistic director.

By late in the summer of 1982 rumors of a split between Baryshnikov and Jessica Lange had begun to circulate. Having recovered from his knee injury, Baryshnikov was dancing again; during ABT's summer layoff he had taken off for the Spoleto Festival in Italy. Lange and their daughter had gone to Minnesota, and they hadn't come back. *Tootsie* was finished; Lange needed time to think. With no phone in her log house she didn't have to answer any questions. When the press finally caught up with her Lange insisted that although she and Misha were apart, they were still together—"I accept the man and the relationship for what they are," she said—but then in 1983 the couple parted for good. Baryshnikov's job was hanging uneasily; Lange had followed her dream.

At different times and in different contexts, Lange and Baryshnikov have both said they don't believe in working on a relationship. If the emotional high isn't there, it's time to quit. Lange's life had been changing rapidly—first a child, then sudden success. She'd grown; her life was full. Things didn't balance out any more. There was no point in conducting a relationship by long-distance telecommunication. She'd bought land near Taos. She didn't need the complications Baryshnikov brought into her life.

Lange's turning point was *Frances*. According to Lange, playing Frances was one of the most intensely emotional experiences of her life. For months she had to maintain an extraordinary level of passion and rage as she portrayed the shipwreck of a woman who cared too much. Whatever she felt, she felt desperately. That was the nature of her role. In the process Lange fell in love with forty-year-old Sam Shepard, the actor and Pulitzer Prize-winning playwright laureate of the American West. Gentle yet strong, Shepard represented Baryshnikov's antithesis. He was an American dreamer with a love of the land, solid and straightforward. Shepard left his wife O-Lan and fourteen-year-old son and moved in with Lange and her daughter.

Later Misha would talk about "the extremes of emotion between people" on movie sets from his own experience with the filming of *White Nights:* "Now I understand why there are so many scandals on sets. People get wild, unpleasant, get into trouble, fall in love."

Misha was desolate. He admitted later that Lange was the only woman he had ever truly loved. "I feel I was married, and I still am in a way. . . . I have a beautiful daughter and I'm a daddy all the time. I think about her every day. She and her mother will always be a part of my life. Nothing can change that." The wound took some time to heal. In the beginning there was bitterness. When, shortly after the split, two-year-old Shura called her father "Sam" by mistake, Misha was visibly hurt and angry. His daughter had become part of another man's family. But Baryshnikov and Lange remain friends and Alexandra occasionally spends a week or two with her father at Sneden's Landing. "She's the one person I have," says Misha. He does not want her to become a ballerina.

"We dancers are very lonely people. We work together but we are very much self-made, self-centered individuals," says Misha. The man who at twenty-nine had spoken of performing as "a form of opium," at thirty as something he would stop doing in three or four years, and at thirty-three as only bread and butter was still dancing at thirty-five. Much of the time he danced in pain; his physical therapist now lived and traveled with the company, and Misha saw him at least once a day. Success seemed sad—not being able to walk his dogs in the park any more, not being able to go to a movie. His dreams of a life in the country had vanished along with his family. Yet he knew they were only dreams, and in a way he despised himself because he was a slave to the spotlight.

In the summer of 1983 the situation at Ballet Theatre looked very serious, and Misha was considering quitting. He was fed up with the struggle and was still pained by the split with Lange. There were a hundred lucrative ventures he could get involved in—he could do guest performances; he could form a small troupe and go to Monte Carlo—he didn't have to put up with the barrage of criticism that was wearing him down, and he certainly didn't intend to change his approach to Ballet Theatre. He needed time to think.

Misha rented a house on the ocean side of Fire Island, close enough to the city so that he could rush back for emergency board meetings, and took his new girlfriend, Lisa Rinehart, with him. Lisa, a dancer in the corps de ballet, was a classic beauty. He wanted to think, but he didn't want to be alone. He couldn't be alone. Later he invited a couple of his protégés and Charles France to join him there, and while they partied he fished in the ocean and brooded over his future. The more options he was faced with, the more Misha seemed to withdraw.

Finally, in the fall of 1983, after a ten-week dancers' lockout, continued critical response from the press, and with a budget deficit of almost two-million dollars, Herman Krawitz was fired, Donald Kendall resigned, and several board members left. Baryshnikov's resignation was rejected, and he agreed to stay on condition that his performance as director be judged independently from where or how much he danced. Since then he has worked without a contract for a handshake and one dollar a year, leaving him free to dance or not to dance wherever and whenever he pleases. As artistic director he has also cut himself off from the press, refusing to read criticism or give interviews about his job. In effect he has said, "I'll do it my way or not at all."

After his first year with the classics at ABT Baryshnikov had begun to dramatically expand the company's repertoire, bringing in original works by modern choregraphers like Twyla Tharp, Merce Cunningham, Kenneth MacMillan, and Paul Taylor and more ballets by Robbins and Balanchine. His company is happier doing Tharp or Taylor than a classic Russian ballet, he says, "because that's what they are—Americans kids." His involvement with new dance choregraphers has excited him, relieving the jaded attitude toward dance that has sometimes gripped him. "I feel like a kid again," Misha said after he'd been working with one young choreographer. As artistic director he has even been able to commission ballets for himself without suffering ethical remorse.

The response has been mixed. While his supporters praise his intellectual courage, Baryshnikov's detractors have accused him of falling for vacuous artsiness and hip sensationalism, particularly in Ballet Theatre's most popular ballets. Misha admits that some of the new ballets have been failures, but he had to try. Sometimes he just didn't know what would and would not work until he heard the response. But in the process he has expanded his own horizons and those of his company while giving crucial support to some intelligent young choreographers. He has also provided ABT with its share of often profitable controversy.

In 1985 Baryshnikov attended a performance by dancer and choreographer Karole Armitage. Hailed as the "punk princess of the downtown scene," Armitage was performing her frenetic *Watteau Duet*; dressed in black leather, high heels, and lacy stockings and dancing to garish noise, she cartwheeled, attacked her partner, and was dragged offstage by her feet. She'd been a big hit in Paris. Her major influences were known to include Balanchine, Cunningham, Buddhist art, Duchamp, Velasquez, and Motown.

After the performance a stunned Baryshnikov burst into the dressing room, where Armitage was just drying off after a shower, and smothered her with hugs and congratulations. Later he drove some friends back to Sneden's Landing and spent the late hours doing interpretations of Armitage. He was hooked. Two weeks later he commissioned her to create a ballet for ABT, with sets and costumes by her fiancé, David Salle, one of the foremost neo-expressionist painters on the American scene.

The Mollino Room was Armitage's answer to Baryshnikov. The ballet was designed as a portrait of Misha and his "loaded cultural icon-like image," as Armitage put it—the Russian brooder. While five couples waltzed together around the stage, Misha danced by himself. He was the sullen loner who couldn't connect with the dancing couples. His movements were cut short, spikey, turned in upon themselves. His legs were knives cutting the air. This was classical ballet, perverted.

"Baryshnikov Goes Punk," proclaimed *Newsweek* in one of the many disparaging reviews of the new ABT ballet. The public thronged to see the new, bad Misha in one of the hippest events of the ballet year. Yet most critics didn't know what to make of it except to admit that it was hip. Certainly, this experiment in bad taste was something new and risqué in the world of ballet, they said, but so what? Ballet loyalists didn't really want to see a great and eloquent ballet dancer perform such disonant choreography. And without him, they said, the ballet would have died. Armitage presented her own line of defense. Talking to *People* magazine on July 21, 1986, she spoke about dance as an art that reflects "how it feels to live." "When you are living in a post-holocaust, nuclear world, I don't think a regal style is appropriate," she said.

Perhaps it was inevitable that the more Baryshnikov branched out, the more he failed in the eyes of those who had once hailed his arrival in the West. The exquisite purity and modest charm of the young Russian who had captured the heart of America was compromised not by his restless search for new styles and frontiers but by the glamorous commercialism which he accepted and sometimes wholeheartedly embraced. The more he tried to cater to American tastes, the more he failed in the eyes of the ballet establishment. His million-dollar *Cinderella*, with its press kit weighing in at almost one-and-a-half pounds and its campy Ugly Sisters, was a critical flop and a public hit. It was all spectacle, said the critics, no substance, a cool ballet with moments of pure corn rather than a romance. It was another product of the "capitalist paradise."

The great Russian star was emerging as an enigma. His simple downtown loft, with its Cocteau pen and ink drawings and its shelves of books and classical music belied the tastelessness he sometimes allowed himself when he stepped into the unfamiliar. As time went by, Baryshnikov's personal sidelines did the most harm to his public image. Those who criticized *The Turning Point* nevertheless praised Baryshnikov's individual performance in the movie; he was new to the game, and he didn't understand the language. The Tony Award–winning "Baryshnikov on Broadway" was popular and innocuous; it was a new arrival's ode to the national tradition. But by the time Misha appeared in the May 1982 television special "Baryshnikov in Hollywood," few were prepared to forgive him. "It's getting a bit tiresome having him cast in the role of the innocent abroad," wrote John Gruen in the May 1982 issue of *Dancemagazine*.

The special, narrated by Orson Welles and starring Gene Wilder and Shirley MacLaine, featured Baryshnikov as the eager young hero whose dreams of movie stardom are thwarted by Hollywood's cruel machinations; he believes that he's going to be a Hollywood actor, but Hollywood is merely using him for his dancing. The fact that Misha was involved in casting, script development, and tape editing made it all the harder for critics to accept the mindlessness of the production and the choreography which, as Gruen said, "sabotages his artistry and diminishes his potential as an actor." The only bit of real acting, said Gruen, was "the recollection of a Russian farewell." The farewell was to his dog.

In 1985 Misha tried again, this time with *White Nights*, a film that tapped America's lingering hunger for the mystique of the

impassioned Russian defector—an image with which Baryshnikov had fired the public imagination ten years earlier. *White
Nights*, directed by Taylor Hackford of *An Officer and a Gentleman*
fame, was conceived as a political thriller with music and dance
video undertones. Hackford was known for movies in which
dance and rock music were an integral dramatic element, and
this time he created his story with two specific dancers in mind:
Mikhail Baryshnikov and Gregory Hines. The two dancers knew
and admired each other's work, but they came from entirely different backgrounds—a Russian from the rarified Kirov and a
black from the streets of New York. The movie also introduced
Isabella Rossellini, famed for her Lancôme commercials and
for being Ingrid Bergman's daughter, in her first English-lan-
guage feature role. Rossellini soon became another of Baryshnikov's rumored romances, although both denied any romantic
involvement.

"Baryshnikov had turned down films time and time again, and
he had refused to film the story of his defection," said Hackford.
So he was surprised when in 1982 both dancers agreed to his
proposal for a movie that casts Baryshnikov in a dangerously
true-to-life role as Kolya, the celebrated Russian defector ballet
star whose airliner crash-lands in Siberia, and Hines in the
touchy role of Raymond, a disaffected black American Vietnam
deserter, a tap dancer who has exiled himself to Russia and is
drawn by the KGB into a plot to make Kolya dance again at the
Kirov Theater. Hackford speculates that the challenge of syn-
thesizing ballet and tap into a new form drew both dancers to
the movie. Unfortunately, not much of that synthesis found its
way into the final product.

"I'm still surprised I got into it," Misha told *People* magazine,
December 16, 1985, after the film's release in November, adding
that its blatantly anti-Soviet tone would probably ruin any hope
of his ever being able to return to his homeland as a visitor
under Gorbachev's promising new regime. During the five

months that he spent on location filming *White Nights*, Misha
came as close to being home as he had been in ten years.

They filmed on the island of Reposaari off the northwestern
coast of Finland, just miles across the water from the Soviet
Union, where the midsummer arctic twilight resembles the
white nights of Siberia. Scenes set in Misha's beloved Leningrad
were shot in Helsinki, Finland's capital city, which has sections
designed by St. Petersburg architects. In an eerie imitation of
real life, Hackford created an apartment almost identical in its
details to the Moika Canal apartment Misha left behind in
1974—and like Misha's, the fictional apartment had been left
undisturbed in anticipation of the dancer's return. Hackford discovered that Lisbon's San Carlos Opera House could practically
double for the Kirov Theater in its feeling of intimacy. "As I
danced the scenes," Baryshnikov told *People* magazine, "I remembered perfectly the last time I danced in Leningrad. . . . It was a
powerful experience." And for one speechless hour Misha
watched as the busy streets of Leningrad, the sidewalks and the
buses and the billboards, even the elegant facade of the building
he'd once lived in rolled across the screen. The raw footage had
been filmed in Leningrad for Hackford. All of the memories that
Misha had kept safely locked away for years returned in waves of
nostalgia.

Misha distanced himself from the production after it was released to reviews that described it as a "mish-mash," "contrived,"
and "naive." Asked why he had accepted the part, he answered
simply, "Why not?" He was embarrassed. The movie is clearly
biographical, right down to a snippet of footage smuggled out of
the Soviet Union showing Misha as a teenager dancing in Pushkin's class, and yet it presents a laughably stereotypical view of
life in the Soviet Union. The action clings to pulp-fiction notions of Siberian salt mines, endless bottles of vodka, swarms of
poker-faced KGB agents, and hidden cameras and microphones
in every corner.

Baryshnikov claimed to have certain "moral responsibilities" to his mother country. Although he was "hired as an actor," which apparently meant that he didn't necessarily agree with the movie, he fought incessantly with Hackford over small details that he considered inconsistent or *klyukva*, "phony." He supposedly went through each draft of the script with a fine-tooth comb, and he coached Hines and Rossellini in the more subtle details of Russian life—from their accents to how Darya would tie her scarf.

Baryshnikov and Hackford fought about the music. Hackford wanted a scene with Misha idly playing the piano; Misha didn't. "He wanted it to sound like Vladimir Horowitz," said Hackford. Baryshnikov didn't want to dance to the passionate folk music of a banned Russian singer; eventually he did, creating a powerful Balanchinesque dance that won back the heart of his former lover, Galina, and became the highlight of the movie. Most of all Baryshnikov objected to the huge cassette player that Kolya drags around, blasting out rock and rap tunes, on the pretext of drowning out KGB bugs: "It was no big deal, but I felt uncomfortable." Hackford had commissioned original music from names such as Phil Collins and Lionel Richie ("Say You Say Me" was the movie's theme song), and he hoped to release excerpts as MTV music videos.

White Nights took a huge toll on Misha, in body and in spirit. Before shooting even began he was coached for two months by Sandra Seacat, Jessica Lange's actor's studio teacher and a follower of Swami Baba Muktananda. Seacat had taught Lange the meditative centering techniques that she used in *Frances*. The classes payed off; especially in Baryshnikov's more caustic moments he played his part well. Then there were the emotionally exhausting arguments; the months spent traveling and filming on location from Finland to Lisbon, Scotland, and England; the living-out of difficult memories and fears. Misha helped himself through these months by thinking about his daughter back home. He was lonely.

Most taxing of all was the filming of dance sequences, some of which were choreographed by Twyla Tharp. Hackford had set himself the technical challenge of filming dance with a moving camera and without cutting, which meant that many sequences had to be shot several times, beginning to end, until they were right from both the dancer's and the camera's point of view. One particularly difficult series of moves—the scene from Petit's *Le Jeune Homme et La Mort* with which the film opens—had to be repeated twenty-six times. And all the time Baryshnikov had to stay warmed up and ready to dance. While everyone else took time off for lunch or coffee, he had to do his exercises. Halfway through filming Misha was seriously thinking about quitting dance. By the end he was in such bad shape that he was having trouble performing.

Baryshnikov claims that it took him six months to get over the trauma of *White Nights*. His company suffered with him. In his absence ABT foundered again, criticism thrived, and the budget deficit grew. He had become the focus of a company that was still trying to establish its new personality. The public still missed the dazzling star power of the old days, and they had mixed feelings about the kids who were now dancing center stage. They didn't know what ABT stood for any more, not least because its shining light, Mikhail Baryshnikov, was nowhere to be seen. The dancers felt abandoned; when they toured Japan he was away filming. Even when he was with them during this period, he tended to be moody, so that an unbearable atmosphere clouded the whole company.

Then, on the last day of July 1985, during a marathon twenty-nine-city performance tour with his summer touring group, Baryshnikov and Co., Misha injured his right knee again. In August he had to undergo arthroscopic surgery to take care of seriously worn and torn cartilage. At the same time, the sheath of his left Achilles tendon was cleaned up. He was out of action for five months, during which time the ballet world sunk into a mire of controversy.

It seemed as if the world could forgive Misha almost anything when they saw him dancing, but when he wasn't dancing the criticism flowed. Now the attacks became personal. As the ballet world divided itself into pro and anti-Baryshnikov camps, a bullet came from Fernando Bujones, whose relationship with Misha had always been ambivalent and competitive. In August 1985 Bujones left ABT in a huff, claiming that Baryshnikov was ruining Ballet Theatre, that he was a cold fish, that as a dancer he had stolen the spotlight, and that as a director he had tried to suppress Bujones—all because Baryshnikov had refused to incorporate into the repertoire a ballet created for Bujones by Maurice Béjart.

Bujones had been criticized for his preoccupation with stardom, yet now his words became ammunition for the forces. As far as the anti-Baryshnikov camp was concerned, it all added up. The artistic director could not deal with another male star in the company. He couldn't take the competition. All of his favored male leads were kids; they were no competition. And as the only male dancer with Baryshnikov and Co., Misha was a lone prince amongst ten hand-picked ABT ballerinas.

Baryshnikov had made a million and injured his knee on his own summer tour, and now he couldn't dance with ABT in New York. There were even suggestions in the local press that he had invited his knee injury as an excuse not to dance during the coming season at the Met. Was Baryshnikov in such bad shape that he couldn't face his audience? ABT, sick of the scandals, was not talking to the press. Board members were under threat of dismissal if they broke their silence, and Misha hadn't been talking since the ABT debacle of 1982. Besides, the subject of injuries has long been taboo in the world of ballet. The illusion, the "beautiful lie," as Misha calls it, couldn't stand up to an audience watching for pain to cross the face of a Russian prince.

Misha was stressed. What with the movie, his responsibilities to ABT, and his summer tour, he'd overloaded his system again.

And once again his body had rebelled, forcing him to sit back, rest his aching muscles, and take stock of the situation. It was becoming a familiar pattern, but it was getting harder to bounce back. Baryshnikov was totally dependent now on the support of Peter Marshall, the physical therapist who three years earlier had given up his private practice to set up office with ABT. "I feel like I am married to him," Baryshnikov said. At least twice a day he waited his turn for therapy in Marshall's office, where during performance season as many as forty dancers a day came to be bandaged, manipulated, or medicated. And whenever Baryshnikov was onstage, Marshall was backstage in his impromptu treatment room, ready for the dancer to come limping into the wings on his exit. Marshall knew every vulnerable part of Baryshnikov's body, and he was by now an expert in on-the-spot, behind-the-scenes repair jobs. But these were quick fixes designed to rescue a performance, whereas Misha was living with chronic pain, both onstage and off.

Misha danced less and less with the company in subsequent seasons and then scarcely at all after 1987. Yet he continued his summer tours with Baryshnikov and Co., dancing through minor injuries and finally canceling eight performances in 1987 after he badly hurt his ankle. Why did he continue to risk injury dancing with his own company but increasingly not with ABT? Baryshnikov claims that by not dancing with ABT he gives the kids more of a chance to be noticed and gives himself the opportunity of watching them perform from the front of the house, which is far preferable to the backstage view he has when he participates in the performance. On the other hand, Baryshnikov and Co. is a personal, money-making venture that depends entirely on Misha's starry presence. The small troupe performs across the nation to crowds of ten thousand or more, filling stadiums and other rock concert venues with enthusiastic fans who are far less demanding than ABT's sophisticated New York audience.

Misha worked with weights, stopped smoking, stopped drinking, stopped partying, changed his diet, and tried to get back in shape. He relaxed just enough to enable him to keep going. He wasn't ready to quit. However much he knew that his life as a dancer was running out, how could he live without the stage, the applause, the lights—all the glamor that had driven him to work at being a dancer way back when he was a boy who could have been out playing gangsters with the other kids. Since then, it was only when he was injured that he knew what it was like to go without. After all, what was he if not a dancer?

SEVENTEEN

Dogs Bark, but Wind Blows It Away

FOR FIVE YEARS Baryshnikov had walked the tightrope between dancing and directing—five years that marked as much of a transition in American ballet as in the life of its most controversial artistic director and its greatest dancer. It had been a stormy period. Balanchine's death in April 1983, the rise of a new, postmodern choreography, the easing of boundaries between various dance forms, the decline of international ballet stars, the immense growth in ballet's popular appeal, and an intense debate over the function of ballet companies in American society (were they custodians or entertainers?)—all of these indicated the coming of a new generation and a new phase in American ballet.

As Misha moved ABT into 1986 it began to dawn on many that not only the company but the whole world of ballet, and the world outside, was inevitably changing and that Baryshnikov, as a dancer, ballet idol, and director, had played an important role in moving American ballet toward its admittedly uncertain future. The time is turn-of-the-century America, postapocalyptic, nuclear, and postmodern. And Misha, with his sometimes uncomfortable mix of Old World and New World, king and jester, loner and extrovert, is a postmodern man.

"His life isn't his own; it belongs to everybody. It's very difficult for him now," says Baryshnikov's former teacher, Bella Kovarskaya. She remembers him as a bright student in her Riga classroom. Now his glossy poster hangs in the corridor of her Toronto ballet school and her students worship him. They dream of becoming stars. Misha laughs because they have no idea what stardom means. Misha has made his millions and with his name he can make many more. He has a partnership with Regis Philbin, co-host of the WABC Morning Show, in a trendy Manhattan restaurant called Columbus, and he has lent his name to license perfumes and a line of exercise clothes. Movie scripts await his attention. He can take his pick from the best that money can buy. But he has lost a life that's free for the taking. That loss, says his friends, has kept him "mad and hungry" enough to keep dancing.

After *White Nights* Baryshnikov began to talk more openly about his life in the Soviet Union. There, he said, to be a dancer was to be a civil servant. One danced for the state. He came to the West because he wanted to dance for himself—although he is too professional to forget that he has to please his audience first. Nevertheless, Misha has danced everything. He has had fantastic choreographic opportunities. Twyla Tharp has created a body of work for him that perfectly mirrors his personality— quirky and urbane, modern and funny, cool and just a tiny bit romantic. If he wants, he can dance for himself. Yet he doesn't belong to himself. He belongs to the American public. Misha, the restless young defector who danced from one stage to another and from one embrace to another has become Baryshnikov, an established figure in the world of American dance and culture.

He has danced for two U.S. presidents, he has dined with visiting royalty, he has hosted and performed in numerous benefits, including several for AIDS. In 1982 he was given the keys to the city of Birmingham, Alabama, and in 1985 he received an honorary doctorate in humanities from the prestigious Columbia University. Behind the scenes Misha has helped a lot of people. He finances Russian émigré publications, he does what he can for others who have just come to America, and he's supportive of young talent.

In 1985 Baryshnikov became a U.S. citizen and the following year he helped organize the historic joint appearance of ABT with Nureyev's Paris Opéra Ballet in a gala performance for the Statue of Liberty celebration in New York City. As he stood with Nureyev on the grand tier of the Metropolitan Opera House to make his joint announcement, there was no doubt that this was a different Misha. Here was an elegant middle-aged man speaking on behalf of his company.

By 1984 Robert LaFosse and Susan Jaffe were full-fledged principals representing a new approach to being a ballet dancer. "Dancers . . . want to be real people leading real lives," LaFosse told *Dancemagazine* in May 1985. Perhaps Baryshnikov has taught his dancers more than he intended. They're committed artists who know that a dancer's life is short, and they want to grow up before it's too late. Misha grew up with his company. It wasn't easy, and it wasn't absolute. At the age of forty he remains a bachelor. He lives alone with his faithful dogs and a house-keeper—an older woman who is almost a mother to him. He has grappled with some personal problems. He takes pride in having shed his bitterness and developed a generous feeling to-ward Jessica Lange and Sam Shepard. He's happy for them. Al-exandra remains the light of his life, his reason for life beyond dance. He's learned to care for his company. He can still be impossible and his own projects still come first, but he can be nurturing, too. Now he finds time to give his chosen kids special care and attention, to joke with them, to consider seriously whether they're ready to deal with the pressures of a full-length ballet and public exposure.

Misha has learned about himself. He admits that he's moody and that when he's down he's intolerable, but he says he's working on it. He has stayed with his company, riding the highs and the lows that have always been a part of Ballet Theatre life. He has witnessed the nervous breakdowns, the frustrations, the downfalls of dancers to whom he is responsible as a boss. He has witnessed the death by drugs of Patrick Bissell, a great young dancer who some say was pushed too far and too fast. He has watched Gelsey Kirkland unravel almost to the point of death. For each tragedy he has been held partly responsible. It has been something of a sobering experience.

Yet perhaps what has matured Misha more than anything else is the daily thought that maybe today, maybe tomorrow, his body will not be capable of serving him in the thing he has always done best. All his life Misha has been as near to perfect a dancer as one can get. Dancing, he has always been the greatest. It's a form of addiction. Misha is unused to imperfection in himself and has not accepted it easily in others. Yet as he confronts himself as a nondancer, or as an imperfect actor or director, he grows warmer. "My ego as a dancer has to be in my pocket," says Misha with a wry smile.

By 1986 Natalia Makarova and Peter Martins had both retired from dance. Misha was still dancing, though no longer in full-length ballets and very little with ABT. He was reserving his energy for ballets that especially excited him—for instance, in 1986 he danced in drag, his first ballerina role, in David Gordon's comic postmodern ballet *Murder*—and limiting himself to roles that would not endanger him physically. Sometimes there was a conflict, such as in 1986, when his doctors advised him not to perform in *Requiem*, a work by Kenneth MacMillan. Baryshnikov felt torn. *Requiem* attracted him for several reasons. Based on a tragic and bloody story of two Cambodian youths it is a ballet of huge emotions and epic scale. A choir of forty accompanies the orchestra and the dance includes dynamic, an-gular movements, jazz, and a break-dance "moon walk." Even without Misha the ballet was a major hit for ABT.

Misha was living with a chronic knee injury, tendonitis, arthritis, and countless aches and pains from overstressed joints. By now he was visiting Peter Marshall's office at least twice a day. He needed three or four massages a week. Because of his arthritis he reportedly had to "crawl to the bathroom" in the morning before forcing his legs to work. He was taking anti-inflammatory medications and his home was fully equipped with ultrasound and electrotherapeutic machines.

Yet he knew he was a smarter dancer now. His Kirov training gave him the facility to fake some painful moves, and he could count on the strength of his presence on stage, his ability to communicate through the slightest shifts of his body. Reviewing his performance as *Swan Lake's* Prince Siegfried for *Dancemagazine* in September 1985 Joan Ross Acocella wrote, "His mere shoulder, seen from behind, told you everything you need to know about the Act III Siegfried: that he's a prince, that he is in love, that he is in doubt."

"There's just not much time left for me to dance," Baryshnikov said as he approached forty. He was cooly measuring his physical decline, and he knew that if he wanted to make a final statement on film it had to be now. It seemed as if the whole ballet world was waiting breathlessly for his last dance. What would he choose? When Baryshnikov danced the ballerina role in Gordon's gothic ballet *Murder* he was asked if this was it—did he plan to end his career in drag? Misha laughed at such a preposterous idea. "If I *was* dancing the last ballet in my life," he told Lewis Segal in the March 2, 1986 *Los Angeles Times*, "maybe I wouldn't choose this one. Maybe I would finish nicely with *Giselle.*"

Misha knew. He knew he wanted to make a permanent record of his favorite ballet, *Giselle*, while he was still able: "It happens that this was one of my first serious roles at the Kirov Ballet. I

danced it through my entire career with different ballerinas."
Misha had grown up in the role. When at age twenty-two he
first assumed the role of Albrecht at the Kirov, the audience was
struck not just by his incredible technique but even more by the
way he had risked a radical reinterpretation of the role. He had
remade Albrecht in his own image—an impulsive young man
swept off his feet by romantic love, a youth driven by passion to
conceal his high rank from the peasant girl Giselle.

At the time he was courting Tanya Koltsova, the Vaganova
student who was hesitant to enter a relationship with a young
star like Baryshnikov. As the grind of life at the Kirov began to
leave its imprint, Albrecht become less innocent. A subtle bitterness emerged. By the time of his last Kirov performance, one
month before his defection, Albrecht had become a figure filled
with tragic desperation. Opposite Gelsey Kirkland's Giselle, Albrecht changed again. Kirkland was emotionally disintegrating
before his eyes, while he was living in a whirlwind; Misha invented his own mad scene.

And now, as he considered his final *Giselle*, here was another
Misha, mature, cool, a little jaded by love and loss. Things had
come full circle. Now he would dance Albrecht in the tradition
of the greatest *danseurs* in ballet history: he was Albrecht the
seducer. "Now, Albrecht looks at Giselle from the distance of
experience," says Baryshnikov. Yet he still couldn't entirely believe in Albrecht as a cynic toying with a girl's innocent love.
"This young girl does trap his imagination completely," he ex-
plains. "It happens to many people: They dream about a person
they consider so extraordinary. It becomes obsessive." In many
ways, *Giselle* was the story of Misha's life.

Baryshnikov approached Herbert Ross and Nora Kaye, who
had directed and produced *The Turning Point*, with his idea for a
straight, beginning-to-end film record of *Giselle*. He had no big
commercial aspirations for the project. Ross was intrigued, but
as a director he wanted more of a challenge. He wanted to put
the camera on the stage, to show the process of making a

ballet—the lights, rehearsals, backstage. He wanted to make a full-length feature movie, and it had to be commercially viable. How could he satisfy these ambitions with a simple record of the ballet? There was also a question as to whether Baryshnikov could safely dance the whole ballet in his worn physical condition. He had filmed enough dance documentaries to know that he would have to dance the whole ballet through several times so that the best takes could be spliced together.

Ross persuaded Baryshnikov that the best solution would be to create a contemporary, parallel story centered around the dancers, in which scenes from the ballet could be intertwined with a dramatic plot. It had been done before: Carlos Saura had succeeded with the same treatment with *Carmen. Giselle* easily had as much potential as a modern romance. "It's a story about human lives that is relevant to audiences today just as it was in the 19th century," says Baryshnikov.

Ross commissioned screenwriter Sarah Kernochan, who had recently co-written the screenplay for *9½ Weeks*, to prepare a script for the story of a troupe of dancers involved in the staging of *Giselle*. The idea was to use ABT dancers both in the ballet scenes and as actors representing the contemporary characters. The drama was to center on Anton Sergeyev (Baryshnikov), glamorous director and ballet star, who is in the process of staging *Giselle* with his company. Partway through rehearsals, Anton is rescued from a mid-life crisis that has sapped his desire to dance by his infatuation with a pretty young dancer in the corps de ballet. The dancer, Lisa (Julie Kent), falls for Anton but discovers that she has been betrayed when Paolo, a young Italian Hilarion who is in love with her, tells her that Anton is already engaged to be married to a countess. In fact, Anton is also involved in a casual affair with Francesca (Alessandra Ferri), the ballerina who dances the part of Giselle. Hurt, Lisa disappears, and Anton, like Albrecht, is shocked into a timely reevaluation of himself that ultimately revives his spirit as a dancer. Unlike Giselle, Lisa does not die. She does forgive the cad Anton on the basis that a few days spent being romanced by him were worth the experience. And of course she forgives him because she loves his art.

Kernochan took the basic story and set to work creating a double parallel—the movie characters would mirror the characters in the ballet *and* the real lives of the ABT dancer-actors. She spent time at the ABT studios, speaking with the dancers involved and developing fictitious characters based on their personalities. She was intrigued to find that Misha had a sympathetic view of Albrecht, that he identified with him closely as a man obsessed by the elusive quality of women. "I'm fascinated by women," Baryshnikov admits. "I'm very curious about the way they're thinking, the way they operate their lives. I love to be next to them; I love to talk to them." And just as Anton is inspired to dance with renewed vigor by the innocent Lisa, so Misha claims woman as his muse: "I've always danced for one person somewhere in the audience. If she's not there, she's in my imagination."

In some respects Kernochan came dangerously close to real life in her characterizations. The scene in which Lisa discovers that she is not the only girl who Anton has compared with the tall white birch trees of his native Russian village recalls a passage in Gelsey Kirkland's autobiography in which she claims that she was not the only girl seduced by Misha's sad tale of abandonment by his mother.

The most ironic parallel of the movie is that between Leslie Browne and the character Nadine, the woman who hates men— especially Anton, who years ago trifled with her still-innocent love for him. The reference to Browne's experience with Yuri/Misha ten years earlier, in and after *The Turning Point*, is played mercilessly throughout the movie. When Lisa first falls for Anton's perfectly played advances Nadine snaps, "You're gonna wish you stayed in the audience." To drive the point home Nadine dances *Giselle*'s man-hating Queen of the Wilis in the ballet scenes.

With the deluded older woman portrayed by Browne, the young victim of Baryshnikov/Yuri/Anton's whim is now Lisa—in real-life Julie Kent. Like Browne, when Kent received her contract for the movie she was only seventeen. Her mother had to sign it. Misha had noticed her a short time earlier when she auditioned for the ABT corps, and he remembered her as an "extraordinary looking girl. I haven't seen a face like that anywhere. I knew if she could act a bit . . ." Perhaps, hoped Misha, that magic would be there.

Giselle, subsequently renamed *Dancers* when Ross discovered that people tended to pronounce it as "gizzle," was shot in 1986 during six summer weeks in the city of Bari, in southern Italy. This time Baryshnikov took ABT with him. While Ross directed the movie, Misha directed his company in the ballet scenes, danced, and acted. Although he didn't dance much, he was on his feet and working eighteen hours a day. There was very little time for conflicts to develop between Ross and Baryshnikov, and very little was discussed. The company had to be back in New York by a fixed date to rehearse for the coming season. Baryshnikov claims he didn't even have the time or energy to watch the dailies.

Near the beginning of *Dancers* Anton says, "This is the last time I will dance." Surrounded by his company, one senses that as director he is both the center and an expendable appendage to a living organism. While the dancers travel together, he comes and goes in his fast sports car just as he comes and goes from his lover Francesca. She doesn't need him, she merely accepts his company. At the end of the ballet he stands onstage, utterly alone. As the credits roll, Lisa has forgiven him and gone, Giselle has forgiven him and returned to her grave, the company is packing up, preparing to leave, and there is Anton, alone with his fast red car waiting and a reawakened desire to dance. Surely he will dance again. What else does he have? "We all want to be loved for what we are doing," Misha once said, "I mean, for what else?" All his life Mikhail Baryshnikov has depended on the applause, the flowers, the handshakes, and the kisses and hugs he has received as a dancer. Onstage he is a star. But the beauty is elusive; it cannot be caught. Offstage the star trembles a little.

"He doesn't give himself away," says Alessandra Ferri. "Very few people know Misha really well." "He does set himself apart, but he's friendly," says Julie Kent. And according to Isabella Rossellini, a friend since they co-starred in *White Nights*, Misha is "a very lone man. And quite sad. Quite sad." "I'm a cynical old witch more than a kid at heart," Baryshnikov chuckles, "but one who believes in romantic situations. Without that, life is hard to imagine."

Dancers was an almost instant failure. It was criticized as being corny, sloppy, silly, contrived, and an unfortunate record of a great career. In half-empty movie houses across the country even Baryshnikov's teenage fans, for whom the movie seemed to have been created, laughed at all the wrong, romantic moments. The only good thing was the dancing itself, about a half-hour of *Giselle* near the end of the movie. The consensus was, if only Baryshnikov had stuck to the ballet. Nothing could beat the willowy, romantic power of *Giselle*.

On three days in November 1987, coinciding with the release of *Dancers*, Baryshnikov appeared on "Good Morning America" for three consecutive interviews with Ron Reagan. They talked about Baryshnikov's life and about his recent critical success dancing for the first time with the Martha Graham Dance Company—an experience that revealed to him a whole new dance language and provided a brand-new challenge. Finally they talked about his dream project, *Dancers*. Baryshnikov fidgeted with a piece of paper, folding and unfolding it. For a performer with twenty years of stage experience he seemed intensely self-conscious.

Reagan was talking about his role as Anton: "Now, you know what people are going to say when they see this movie," Reagan was saying. "They're going to say, he's a bit of a skirt-chaser.

They're going to say, That's Misha." Baryshnikov fidgeted. "No," he said with an almost imperceptible shrug. "It's not me at all." He had never actually experienced a crisis like Anton's, he said. He was almost forty and he barely knew himself yet. But it didn't matter. He didn't care what people said about him any more—not as much as he used to, anyway. There is a Russian saying that Baryshnikov likes to quote: "Dogs bark, but wind blows it away."

By then Gelsey Kirkland had barked: her best-selling autobiography was being read by Baryshnikov fans across America. And while Baryshnikov claims not to have read the book, he must have been aware that *Dancers* was not the wind that would blow away Kirkland's cruel and hurtful portrayal of him as a scheming cad, a real-life Albrecht to Gelsey's frail Giselle.

Baryshnikov had invested his name, his company, and countless hours of extremely precious time in *Dancers* for a fraction of the salary he may have received elsewhere. Although he said that it was really Ross's movie, it was always largely Baryshnikov's movie. "I'm scared to death," he admitted in an on-set interview. "The elements are there, and it's an honest attempt, but if I miscalculate. . . ."

Baryshnikov distanced himself from the character Anton and from the movie after its release, just as he had distanced himself from Yuri and *The Turning Point* and from Kolya and *White Nights*. At no time, neither on "Good Morning America," nor in a television interview with Barbara Walters, nor in any interview in print, no matter how hard his hosts attempted to give him the opportunity, did Baryshnikov actively promote *Dancers*. His reticence was so extreme it was almost bewildering.

One Sunday in January 1987 Yuri Grigorovich, the artistic director of the Bolshoi Ballet, went to meet Baryshnikov at a mutual friend's home in New York. It had been thirteen years since their last meeting in Moscow. The last time, Baryshnikov had asked Grigorovich to take him into the Bolshoi. This time Grigorovich, who had come to arrange the first Bolshoi performances in the United States since 1979, was asking Baryshnikov to dance as a guest with the Bolshoi in February. News of the official invitation surprised the world. Headlines proclaiming "Ballet Bombshell" and lengthy analyses of this unprecedented political initiative rolled off the presses as Baryshnikov quietly pondered. "I'll think about it," was all he had said, although it was something he had wished for since his first days in the West.

In the beginning he'd wanted it because he was homesick; he missed his city, his theater, his audience. Now he wanted to show his country what could be achieved by combining a Russian background and education with the kind of creative freedom offered in the West. So he decided to take a gamble. He knew that although his name had disappeared from books, he was still a ballet idol and therefore good public-relations currency in his homeland—why else would Gorbachev risk alienating the hardliners who still considered him a nonperson, a traitor? He also knew that he wanted to take American Ballet Theatre to Russia, to show off his company and introduce his kids to the cradle of classical ballet. He made a deal. He would dance with the Bolshoi in February if he could return with his company in October. When Soviet authorities dithered over the suggestion, excusing themselves with October renovations at the Bolshoi, Baryshnikov told the press: "What every Russian knows is how to stand on line. I guess we have to stand on line to get a theater." More than one year later he was still waiting.

From his home in the West Misha has watched a new generation in Soviet ballet open its doors to this century, accepting ideas and styles that were previously taboo. When, in 1987, Baryshnikov and Nureyev performed in the Martha Graham Dance Company gala, the legendary Bolshoi prima ballerina Maya Plisetskaya was performing, too. And in 1988 two young Bolshoi dancers made an unprecedented appearance performing Balanchine as guests of the New York City Ballet. Only one year earlier it would have been too fantastic to even imagine a Russian star gracing the same stage as two major defectors, or Soviet dancers being permitted to perform the "degenerate" works of Balanchine, another lost son.

Had Misha boarded the bus outside the O'Keefe Center in Toronto instead of running for his life, he would have had to wait more than a decade to satisfy some of his deepest ambitions. He may have danced longer and damaged his body less— or he may have gone the way of Soloviev and Lapauri. He knew all of this when he left his country, saying that things would change but he couldn't wait.

"I am American in everything that I have, but I have a Russian heart. You cannot replace this," Misha once said. There is a scene in *White Nights* in which a Russian tells Kolya, "In America, you are a curiosity, a momentary fad. . . . In a few years you're a has-been. Here, you are a cultural hero." Will Misha be remembered in America like Sinatra and Astaire and Elvis are remembered? In a culture whose heroes have always touched at the heart of the American experience can a ballet dancer become a cultural hero? Perhaps Baryshnikov himself has made this possible; he has given ballet a place in the American heartland. Misha has become both popular idol and legend. In Russia, where great dancers are gods, Misha could have been ensured a glorious place in the history of culture. The name Baryshnikov would resonate in the national imagination long after his final bow. And he could have been certain that future Vaganova students would find a record of his art in the little museum on the fifth floor of the school on Rossi Street. But Misha hasn't danced "like the wind of heaven" for history's sake. He's a pragmatist, and life is short.

Index

206